DECODING YOUR KINK

GUIDE TO EXPLORE SHARE AND ENJOY YOUR WILDEST SEXUAL DESIRES

Galen Fous, MTP

DECODING YOUR KINK

GUIDE TO EXPLORE SHARE AND ENJOY YOUR WILDEST SEXUAL DESIRES

Galen Fous, MTP

Copyright 2015 Galen Fous, MTP
ISBN 10: 1518659535
ISBN 13: 978-1518659539

Cover Design – Galen Robert Fous
Cover Photo – Anonymous

Accolades for Decoding Your Kink

"Galen Fous is a visionary, providing a clear and courageous roadmap for anyone looking to undo the shackles of societally induced sexual shame and go on a journey to discover his or her own Personal Erotic Myth."

Dr. Michael Aaron, NYC Sex Therapist in private practice

"Galen Fous offers a deeply philosophical and spiritual dimension to the phenomenological experience of being kinky...his wisdom is a resource for many who fear, suppress and hide their sexuality due to shame."

David J. Ley, Ph.D.,
Author of 'The Myth of Sex Addiction'

"Shame reduction and self-honesty is at the core of personal liberation, and this is nowhere more true than in sexuality. In this unique and cutting edge book, Galen Fous helps the reader find more clarity about the nature of their hidden sexual truths, and ways to consciously explore their sexual psychology."

Gwenn Cody, LCSW

"Nobody struggles more with the feeling that their erotic desires are 'wrong' or 'broken' than the man or woman who otherwise fits easily into mainstream culture - the heterosexual man and woman into dominance and submission and BDSM. 'Decoding Your Kink' is worth its weight in diamonds to such strugglers, offering them a sensible and nurturing path to self-knowledge, self-acceptance and the erotic intensity we all crave and too few ever obtain."

Janet W. Hardy, co-author of
'The Ethical Slut,' 'The New Bottoming Book,' and more

"In this masterful book, Galen Fous lays out a clear roadmap to unlock your kinky erotic spirit. Concise, beautifully written, techniques and practices to become more present, embodied, and mindful in your relationships, Decoding Your Kink, is an essential guide to those both questioning and well-entrenched in the kink world. Highly recommended."

Jaeleen Bennis, Creator & Founder of Bondassage®,
co-author of 'Bondassage: Kinky Erotic Massage Tips For Lovers'

"Galen Fous smooths the path and leads you through the predicaments, pleasures, enticements and outrageous glories of Kink. His genuine, unique voice is outstanding and heartwarming. A must read!"

Limor Blockman, Ph.D., Clinical Sex Therapist

"Galen Fous' unique insights on a subject much maligned and misunderstood is a primer for individuals interested in exploring the world of kink. It provides guidelines, case studies and personal experiences to assist the reader in shedding their shame and discovering their authentic sexuality."

Susana Mayer, Ph.D., Clinical Sexologist

"At the heart of *Decoding Your Kink*, there stirs an unshakable drive to empower its readers to embrace their authentic selves with honesty and empowered compassion. Fous delivers a compelling thesis that being sexually aware, genuine, honest, and consensual are the greatest gifts we can give unto ourselves and others."

Matt Dobbs,
Managing Director of the Alternative Therapists Directory

"Galen Fous is a pioneer in shameless erotic experience. He makes it safe for anyone who desires to unburden and unleash their sexual energy into a world of untamed exploration. He is serious about his dedication to people's transformation and so is this book. If you want to discover and then play by your own rules, this book is for you."

Laurie Handlers, MA,
Sex and Happiness Coach, Author, & Talk Show Host

"Decoding your Kink by Galen Fous is a groundbreaking book for all to fully explore and find acceptance and wholeness within their own sexuality. In today's world understanding and integrating our sexuality provides a framework for us all to build deep intimate relationships with ourselves and lovers. Galen's research supports that no matter who we are, we all have are kinks and they are "normal". Highly recommended reading for those who desire to explore deeply..."

Kirsteen A. Farley, Somatic Sexologist & Sex Educator

"Galen Fous is a ground-breaking pioneer whose work in sexuality sets free the human spirit from the miasma of fear and shame cloaking our authentic and full expression as sexual beings in this world. His book *Decoding Your Kink: Guide to Explore, Share and Enjoy Your Wildest Sexual Desires* helps you examine, understand, and respect what you value as your true sexual nature, keeping you mindful that your values should be your own."

Jacsman, Sex Life Educator

"Decoding Your Kink is a book written from the heart and one which should be of great help to many people. It encourages a more honest discussion of sexual desire that could help to blow away old and unhelpful prejudices and avoid pejorative labels about Kink oriented sexuality."

Professor Frederick Toates, Open University, England,
Author of 'How Sexual Desire Works: The Enigmatic Urge'

Acknowledgments

Now that I can look back over 6 decades, I see that my life has been immersed in a never-ending flow of love and support. Even at my most desperate, desolate moments when I felt I was failing, abandoned and with no hope of redemption or survival, this long miraculous stream of lovely people came along often just in time, and carried me along and lifted me up. To all of you, and the mystery of life itself, I owe and feel the deepest gratitude.

This book is for you, my Angeluna. For standing beside me, for having my back, being my muse, serving me royally, and loving me like no other. Nothing can sever your soul from my heart.

Table of Contents

World Wide Eros   1

My Personal and Professional Journey into Kink   6

Fear of Your Sex Creature   19

Sex is Friction – Eros is a Myth   27

How to Welcome Your Sex Creature   39

What is an Erotic Mythos?   47

Archetypes, Symbols and the Mythic   57
Psychological Structures of D/s- BDSM

Anatomy of a Personal Erotic Myth   77
Part 1 – A Couple's Journey

Anatomy of a Personal Erotic Myth   83
Part 2 – Her View

Anatomy of a Personal Erotic Myth   90
Part 3 – His View

Why Matching Erotic Myths are   96
Important to Successful Relationships

Take the Discover Your Personal Erotic Myth Survey   100

Love Romance and Kink   105

Is the Problem Sex/Porn Addiction   117
or Sexual Dishonesty?

Healing Sexual Shame, Resolving Sexual Shadows   123

The Body Mirrors Your Inner State   135

MyYoga/OurYoga – A Personal Practice   149
to Gain Presence and Connection

Integrating Your Sexual and Public Persona   153

The Next Steps   158

Fetishsexuality as an Authentic Sexuality   172

WORLD WIDE EROS
KINK, SACRED-SEXUALITY, AND EVERYTHING IN BETWEEN

The "normal" range of human sexual expression is shifting profoundly.

Millions of people around the world have already crossed the thresholds of previous cultural, moral and spiritual norms for acceptable sexual behavior. Millions more stand at their own thresholds, hesitant but eager to cross over. This mass excursion into the full spectrum of Erotic expression is unprecedented in the history of civilization.

New relationship styles are emerging, around a diverse range of sexual orientations and identities. Some join together to express and explore every range of kinky perversity imaginable. Others seek connection through a spiritual path of ecstatic awareness, channeling their sexual "energy" to achieve advanced states of consciousness. On the whole, all of them embrace romantic and loving relationships, but with a few twists!

These early-adapters are exploring the wilderness of the Erotic psyche that has been taboo, forbidden, inappropriate and off-limits to the general population of every era since the rise of "civilization" and organized religion.

These newly emerging aspects of human sexuality are like a gold mine, buried deep within, that culture, religion, morality, superstition, law and fear has kept hidden for millennium. Thanks to the anonymity offered by the Internet, people are digging for and finding this gold deep within their long neglected sexual psyche. They are learning to express and share their sexuality in conscious, ecstatic ways with others. Sexuality is finally being embraced and recognized as an integral aspect of the human experience, at least by an emerging sex-positive culture.

Our Erotic nature is a vast territory, largely unexplored and unmapped. The rich allure of Eros is the promise of great sex. While the allure is an irresistible, lusty come-on, it is just the gateway to our fullest Erotic expression. No matter how dark or perverse, or light and spiritual you seek to be, there are new maps being created and older ones resurrected, that offer the opportunity to express your authentic sexual desire in a healthy, conscious manner.

This new era of Eros gives us all the opportunity to:

- *Communicate honestly and negotiate openly with our partners about our sexual desires;*
- *Consensually express, embody and engage our darkest or lightest Erotic edges;*
- *Resolve the inevitable psychological wounds of sexual repression, trauma and shame our cultures, religions and family embed in us;*
- *Learn techniques to be more fully present, aware, conscious, loving, embodied, enlivened, connected, and intimate;*
- *Cultivate our authentic sexuality as a sacred liberating personal experience;*
- *Develop tolerance and give support and encouragement to those on other sexual paths;*
- *Learn to integrate our liberated sexual being into our everyday cultural, family and spiritual life.*

In other words, the opportunity to live our lives as if our sexuality is NORMAL!!

This shift within the range of human sexuality is significant then, not just for the wild Erotic ecstasy it offers, but also for the potential it has to expand all aspects of being human. Exploring our personal Eros fully, discovering all that has been hidden in the shadows all these years, can lead to a state of greater self-awareness and confidence. Confronting and resolving old shame and guilt can lead to psychological breakthroughs personally, and of course, allow you to achieve the kind of mind-shattering orgasms or wild taboo fetish ecstasy you always fantasize about!

Besides the early-adapters, millions more sex-hungry neophytes are paused at the threshold of their own sexual desire. They want to enter, but are still not quite sure it can be safe, or won't lead their life to ruin. The vivid and visceral reports coming back from the emerging Erotic outposts, sordid and ecstatic both are irresistible. Via the Internet, movies, TV shows, DVD's, books, workshops, events and personal dating sites and apps, a barrage of delicious imagery and opportunity is striking the hungry sexual psyche. This is Eros at its irresistible, alluring best.

But there are definitely cautions and sensibilities to consider as you begin to explore. The explosion of liberated sexuality within the human psyche is still in a very adolescent state. At this early stage, we and those we engage can still be quite immature, reckless, and irresponsible with these compelling opportunities to experience the depths of Eros.

The sexual frontier before us is equivalent to the Wild West before law and order was established. This is the place where the greenhorn can be fleeced, or even harmed accidently, or otherwise. To a great extent, we collectively lack the social and psychological tools and education to communicate and operate honestly about sex. We drag our unresolved shadows, ignorance and wounded parts from our developmental sexual experiences into territory that requires mature, responsible, accountable, well-informed adult behavior.

Many who are paused at the threshold of their sexual desire are held in check by numerous unconscious, sex-negative, shaming beliefs and messages embedded since birth: "Sex is dirty. Men only want one thing. A woman who wants sex is a slut. Good girls/boys don't do that. Don't touch yourself down there. That desire is sick, unnatural, inhuman, evil. It's a sin. You'll go to hell."

We likely have hundreds of these messages clanging away in our unconscious. The closer we get to crossing the threshold of our desire, the louder and more frantic these resistant parts of our psyche can become. The internal fears, judgments and shames they stir up quite often hold the emotional and somatic power to turn us back, shut us down or disconnect us from our quest. Even when we are intellectually aware of them, and understand what we truly desire, such unconscious saboteurs can still deflate our desire.

These internal fear syndromes create "Reefer Madness" style horror stories in our minds. They assault our most vulnerable desires with lurid tales of the ruinous outcomes that await us down the path of our Eros. These subconscious horror myths may leave us feeling emotionally disconnected, frozen, embarrassed, or ashamed about our sexuality. This causes many to postpone, delay, hold back, or cancel their personal Erotic journey all together.

But because our particular sexuality is such an inherent and compelling part of who we are, we will be continually brought back to the yearning of our authentic desire. Eros refuses to be denied!

Even for those who have found the courage to cross the threshold, these old messages and inhibitions can be dragged along. They will still show up again and again, even when we are making progress down the path. Ultimately these culturally embedded, sex-negative messages are calling to be addressed and resolved in some way. The opportunity to face and resolve these old, unwanted messages is one of the many blessings Eros holds for those willing to step deeper.

Our Erotic nature, and all entangled with it, is clearly complex territory. Having at least a rudimentary map of the Erotic wilderness can be helpful. Like any wilderness area, this can be rough territory, with hazards and pitfalls easily catching the uninitiated. There are also unprecedented wealth and riches to be found for ourselves, and our intimate relationships. Pristine oases of sensual delight, rapturous fusion with the divine, sublime Sadeien decadence, and kinky demons and wild sexy beasts of every stripe await those willing to explore.

I have been a guide into the Erotic wilderness for others, and myself for over 15 years. It is where I have chosen to live, learn, make my bed, and trek as far into the terrain as I am able. From this direct experience, my independent sex research studies, and working with hundreds of clients as a sex-positive Transpersonal therapist, I have begun to map this fascinating uncharted terrain. This map is still rough, but clear about many things any explorer will likely encounter in their own inner sexual journey.

My intention is to encourage you to risk your own personal exploration and to help you be risk aware. I also hope to illuminate the many aspects that lay deeper into the terrain, things to keep an eye out for, to notice what may be right beneath your feet, between your or another's legs, within your heart, or high overhead. You may reach forks in the road, where you have to make a choice, or even backtrack.

I hope to offer some fundamental insight into what may lie to the left or right, above or below, or whether to move to the light or the dark, as both may be compelling. But ultimately, this empowering journey is meant for you to explore and draw your own personal map.

My Personal and Professional Journey into Kink

I have been kinky and sexually aware since well before puberty. I know I am not alone in that regard.

I first noticed my sexuality at five years old. I had already picked up the cues that sex was taboo. I hid my interest and curiosity right from the start. I would sit unobtrusively on the floor within a room of grown-ups at holiday gatherings, observing things that interested me from that vantage point. This is where I started my fascination for nylon legs. It was the 1950's and women young and old wore high heels, nylons and garters beneath their tight dresses. I snuck yearning looks at those nylon legs as they sat, got up, walked by. I was an undetected voyeur. I was very turned on. There seemed to be a distinct sexually aware part of my consciousness operating, far beyond my 5 year olds capacity.

Sometimes when these nylon legs sat or stood up I could see a little farther into that dark forbidden zone between them. The ambiguous potential there felt breathtaking. Sometimes I would go to the sofa, from where a woman had risen, and lay my head down in the depression like I was napping. I could feel the warmth of her behind against my cheek, and an aroma that I breathed deeply. I was so enticed by the nectar of a woman's intoxicating scent. More sophisticated sexual pleasures weren't readily available at the age of five!

It might seem surprising, but many people report being engaged in sexual fantasy and masturbation well before the biological trigger of puberty. The premise that Erotic desire does not begin at puberty and is not driven by the reproductive urge is significant for at least a certain portion of the human sexual spectrum. My own research survey of over 2000 participants and many other reporting's indicate a portion of the gene pool's sexual yearnings are driven by symbolic, archetypal, mythic Erotic storylines unrelated to procreative urges or straight-up friction sex. I believe these are indications of an emerging sexual identity and orientation I term 'Fetishsexuality.' I will elaborate on this premise throughout the book.

From the time I was nine, or so, I was in a constant state of arousal. I sought the mysteries of the female at her most seductive in imagery on TV shows, magazines, comic books and the classroom. I began masturbating on my sister's dolls, fantasizing about them as real girls I knew. The dolls were quite small and ill equipped, but I had a huge imagination!

Before puberty, I experimented with and perfected the use of my Dad's shop vac in the basement. That versatile appliance could send me reeling into intoxicating orgasms, even before I could ejaculate. I would damn near pass out from the ecstasy. (I know this was nonconsensual sex and it was wrong, I just didn't know any better at the time! My apologies to Sears and the whole Craftsman family.)

I couldn't wait to have my first ejaculation. When it finally "came", I was ecstatic and relieved. I was now armed and dangerous. I swelled with pride and joy for my deliverance into the wild jungle of male animal prowess, at least as a suddenly pubescent 1960's era boy experiences it!

When I was about 12, I can still remember my father's attempt to explain the facts of life to his only son. It was 1962. I could see how excruciatingly awkward he felt at the task. After his brief technical duty was accomplished, I felt I had confirmed my belief that my mother was still a virgin! I thought this with some potential for fact. My sister and I were both adoptees.

What he told me that day had no impact on my understanding of my sexuality whatsoever. I was way beyond any stingy details he might have dispassionately conveyed. I was already deeply, secretly and instinctually into my own sexual passions and fantasies.

By 13 I knew I was into BDSM when I discovered magazines my brother-in-law kept in the bottom drawer of a bench in his garage. I was snooping around. When I opened the drawer I saw the cover of a magazine with a pic of a young female, mousetraps clamped tightly on her nipples, her lips wrapped succulently around a rubber ball gag, looking into the camera, and right at me, in a most demure way. Her gaze instantly activated something in me that was there already, but beyond my imagination before that moment. This image was tapping into my true authentic Eros – awakening my "sex creature" as I sometimes call it! My first thought was, "Where can I find a girlfriend like this?

At the same time, I lived in terror that my secret sex life might be discovered. I suffered from the intense repression demanded of these instincts and pleasures by my Catholic upbringing. The fear, shyness, and shame of revealing my desires to others as a young boy, kept my true sexual nature hidden deep in shadow. This secrecy strained my psyche and my soul.

As an adult, I carried on my mission, to find "a girl like that." I sought after my kindred soul mate in Kink for the next 30 years…in secret! That is how long it took me to embrace and no longer hide what I had always been. I always hoped I would find the woman of my dreams and erotic fantasies, without having to say directly that is what I was seeking. I was too shy and desperately afraid of how my potential partners, my family, friends and community would judge my sexual desire for Kink.

My "sex creature" felt like a total alien within the Catholic culture I grew up in. I could never imagine that I would ever publicly acknowledge it. It seemed impossible. It was safer to hide and fantasize about what I desired than to proudly claim my true nature – my normal!

Getting turned on by and opening to our edgier desires is just the start of a complex yet enriching journey into the depths of our personal Eros. To fully embrace our edgiest desires and get to the core Eros that is driving us so compellingly is not necessarily an easy, out-of-the-box journey. It can be complicated even if we have the intention to do so in a healthy, conscious, mature and safe way. Let's not leave out the added complexity that another's sexuality and all else that may be entangled with it, is joining us in this dance of Erotic souls.

My personal journey into authentic sexual expression from the sacred to profane continues to deepen, satisfy and astound me.

I have lived my personal life 24/7 as an Erotic Dominant since 1998. This means my relationships, long term and casual are always and only with women who identify as submissive and are interested in consensual Kink with a Dominant man. If you are on Fetlife.com you can find a more personal view of my lifestyle on my page GalenFous-MTP. Send me a friend request if you like. You will need to register to access the site.

I am still wildly celebrating my liberation as a highly sexual, sensuous, kinky man, 24/7 for nearly 2 decades now! The details of my tumultuous liberation from hiding my Kink desires in my late 40's, and the four amazing women who I initially journeyed with are documented in my first book, *The Sharp Edge of Love*, published in 2000.

Since 1998, I have continued to merge desire with lifestyle and profession – as a fetish-positive Transpersonal psychotherapist, sex-positive author, university lecturer, sex-researcher and innovative sex-toy inventor.

The latter refers to the 3-in-1 *Tetruss Portable Dungeon, Suspension Bondage Rig and Sex-Swing* – the world's most versatile adult toy! I designed and began selling the Tetruss in 2000. It is still being sold the world over! You can check it out at Tetruss.com.

Along the way, I returned to academia and finished my Master's degree in Transpersonal Psychology. My graduate thesis allowed me to be immersed in the research, exploration and initial mapping of the mythic, symbolic, archetypal, instinctual, unconsciously embedded aspects of Kink driven Eros I call Fetishsexuality.

One of the highlights of my professional journey into Kink was my 10-year stint as one of the few het-male pro Dom's in the lifestyle. This was an immersion and education into the depths of the sexual psyche few get to experience. Borrowing techniques I learned from intensive study of other modalities I engaged during that time – shadow work, neo-Tantra, mindfulness, somatic body work, conscious movement, depth psychology and more, plus my own insights into Kink dynamics in relationship, I helped client's learn to consciously express and experience the Fetish driven personas that inhabited their desires. As well they learned about presence and embodiment, and how be in integrity with their negotiated agreements. This work would inevitably include working through shame, fear, past traumas and harsh internalized judgments that interfered with their desire.

I retired from being a Pro Dom in 2008 and developed a professional sex-positive counseling practice in Portland, OR and via *Skype* for individuals and couples seeking support in navigating the realms of D/s-BDSM. The focus is on supporting clients to understand and embrace their authentic sexuality and begin to resolve all that resists it. I developed my Conscious Kink workshops held throughout the US starting then as well.

Currently I present at professional conferences, universities and grad schools of psychology, and give media interviews about Sexual Honesty, Sexual Authenticity and Conscious Kink all over the U.S.A and internationally. I am soon planning to launch a syndicated advice column called The Fetish Sex Advisor.

I have had the opportunity to support hundreds of women, men and couples wishing to embrace their sexual desires. It has been my honor to work with them to untangle, understand, come to terms with, communicate openly, define consensual agreements and boundaries, and learn presence, intention, empowerment and healing, in order to express their sexuality in its most honest embodiment.

All of these experiences over the years are gathered in this book to offer insight and guidance to those stepping into the exploration of their own Kink and Fetish desires.

I believe that whatever anyone's sexual truth is, when conducted in a conscious, negotiated, consensual way is entirely NORMAL! I hope this book will inspire those who read it to find their own path to sexual freedom, ecstasy, empowerment and healing.

I will offer no prescriptions or dogma per se for anyone to follow, just a basic map of the very intricate Erotic mindscape.

My desire is to support you to find your own path, your own truth and your own unique way of expressing your Kink yearnings.

My intention is to help you understand that your Kink is absolutely normal…for you!

I intend as well to offer a variety of alternative views, theories and therapeutic approaches that may contrast sharply with current clinical, social, political, religious and moral views of human sexuality. This would include: updating our outdated cultural dating protocols that inhibit forthright sexual honesty about desires; encourage negotiating consent and boundaries; help reduce disastrous erotic mismatches in long term relationships, for a start.

I intend to do whatever I can professionally to establish Fetishsexuality, aka Kink or D/s-BDSM as a valid, definitive sexual identity in clinical, political, academic, social and legal settings. This would include the development of a supportive treatment model for individuals and couples designed around the premise that humans should be encouraged to express their sexual truth. This treatment model would offer practices to untangle fear, shame or harsh self-judgment from people's natural innate, inherent sexual desire at the physical, emotional and cognitive levels.

This book will include methods to enhance your connection physically, emotionally and psychologically to yourself and your partner(s). It will offer techniques to expand your sense of presence and embodiment. There will be guides to help untangle the shames, anxieties, and internalized judgments we inevitably acquire, growing up in a sex-negative culture, one that interferes with our pleasure of sexual expression.

There are in-depth examinations of the many aspects of Kink as they relate to one's personal journey, as well as for couple's in relationship. Included are case studies from my client files and situations you will likely encounter on your own journey. Some of the core concepts of the model I use with clients as well as my personal approach to Kink are complex and nuanced. They will be reiterated in different chapters to highlight and expand the many facets important to the whole experience of your sexual desires.

While I write from a straight male POV, my writings on Kink are primarily generalized, and can apply to anyone of any orientation or gender identity seeking to express their sexuality in a conscious healthy way.

My natural skill set and personal lifestyle is as a hetero-normative, non-poly male. The hetero-normative perspective is a seldom heard, if not a taboo perspective within the burgeoning sex-positive community. I feel that the community is just beginning to awaken to the freedom to be as Kinky as they really are. So I intend to bring the het perspective into the conversation. I hope combined, these views can be supportive for new people just beginning to explore their kinks and for those more experienced in the lifestyle, encountering their edges.

There are a pantheon of sexual identities, orientations and communities emerging on the sexual landscape that began in the early 1950's. In the last 20 years this range of sexual definition and the boundaries of "normal," have been blown off the charts. The public advocates from these pioneering groups are leading the charge towards sexual freedom for everybody.

Having been part of these magnificently diverse Fetish and Sacred Sexuality communities for well over a decade, I am confident we are all not so different. I feel the territory of conscious, negotiated, consensual, risk aware sexual expression and ecstatic engagement is very similar for any orientation. To the greatest extent what I write about or offer could apply to anyone.

Sexuality has been the bastard of human personality for millennia. It has been left in the closet, the back-ally, and on the other side of the tracks. It has been left unexamined as an integral aspect of the human psyche by science, culture and religion.

I have spent nearly 2 decades researching what I call the Erotic Wilderness area of Kink. One key tool in my independent research into what I define as Fetishsexuality is the innovative and groundbreaking *Discover Your Personal Erotic Myth Survey*. This 40 question survey, with over 2000 participants so far, is one of the few research studies into the depths of the sexual unconscious. If you are curious and support this type of research, I invite you to take the ongoing completely anonymous survey at GalenFous.com/PEM. Details about the survey are provided in a later chapter, and on the website.

It is clear that human sexuality is emerging across the globe as the new frontier of human personality. There is no turning back. I am excited to be participating in this unprecedented era of sexual awakening. My prime directive is to help people embrace the full range of their authentic sexual desire and untangle all the shame, fear and traumas that have held their desire back.

The premises, tools and techniques I have developed to support others in this untangling process, are not things taught to academically, clinically trained psychologists, therapists, and marriage and family counselors.

I can forthrightly say, I have become one of America's leading authorities on the nature, psychology and theoretical underpinnings of Fetish, D/s-BDSM and Kink sexuality, from a heterosexual POV. By default, at least! This is virgin territory few are taking a serious look at.

There are few academic institutions that teach, study or view Fetish or Kink driven sexuality as anything but an odd perversion if not an outright pathology, rather than just one's normal sexuality that is distinct from others.

Therapists are not required to explore their own sexual desires nor the inner judgments or projections they may place on clients. They are not required to have examined or resolved the ways their own sexuality may have been traumatized, denied or repressed, from immersion in a sexually immature culture. Yet they are sanctioned as the "qualified" providers of sex therapy by government, mental health institutions and insurance providers. The academic and clinical psychological institutions are about 25 years behind the curve in understanding this explosion of sexual expression, as well as what is needed in a therapeutic sense. (Check out my 4 part lecture to psychology students at Portland State University – Redefining Sex Therapy for 21st Century Sexuality.) There are many great therapists who have the personal skills to support their clients and do so with the gratitude of their clients. The issue is more institutional than personal, and that is a slow wheel to turn.

Human sexuality is still a great and vast wilderness area of psychology. We hardly allow ourselves to look at it, personally or professionally, except in sneaky or shy glances. This keeps the territory of Eros dark, obscure, and out of view. This is certainly proper in its way, but it is also concealing, and giving cover to the destructive shadows of our sexual expression.

Because we do not know how to be honest about our desires with our partners, we often choose instead to sneak, hide, repress, deny, project, and do other harmful behaviors that damage the soul, and ultimately all our relationships.

This has been the state of human's relationship to our natural sexuality for millennium.

Isn't it absolutely insane, that something as obviously pervasive as our sexuality, does not see the light of day, does not get put under the microscope, does not get studied with the same serious scrutiny and intent to understand it, as every other aspect of life on earth?

I am confident that I can speak honestly and knowledgably about Fetishsexuality based on an all around consideration and experience few others have had. And still, I have just barely crossed the frontier of this vast, complex intricate territory. The deeper exploration is before us, both for ourselves, and for our psychological community's comprehension of this tantalizing slice of the sexual pie.

One thing I know clearly. I have found it is possible, with the right fundamental understanding and connection with my partners, to regularly take epic, ritual, mythic journeys into the edgiest, most taboo aspects of our desires. This has opened access to mind and limit-shattering orgasms, ecstatic embodiment of inherent fetish personas such as Dom/sub, Master/slave, Daddy/daughter, rapist/victim and more from the pantheon of archetypes in the collective mindscape, as well as connecting with the most profound depths of intimacy, vulnerability, honesty, and trust imaginable.

Believe me, you do not want to go through life another minute, and be missing out on this glorious potential and fulfillment of your Erotic spirit. And deep down, you know you have no choice. Your authentic desire is with you for life! It will not go away. It will continue to demand your attention…one way or the other!

My personal liberation extends into my everyday life, 24/7. No more sneaking, hiding, lying, or being scared shitless about getting caught by someone I was desperately hiding my Kinky desires from.

My computer hard-drive, browser history, bookmarks, desktop and open Safari tabs are littered with evidence of my porn trail into to every back-alley, and musty dungeon of perversity and sexual oddity imaginable. Hell, I am even in some of them! Nothing is hidden about any aspect of my sexually honest lifestyle.

Not giving a dam who might stumble across the true expression of my sexuality has been a monumental transcendence of my internal fear and shame.

It is a human tragedy that there are so few of us on earth who dare to make this liberated stand as sexually authentic and freedom seeking human beings. Our cultures, governments, religions and families make most of us terrified of ever letting others know our sexual truth. With threats of excommunication, ostracization, criminalization, having a mental disorder, getting fired, going to hell, and monumental public shaming, it is too huge a risk for most.

But your authentic desire will never go away!

I want everyone to be able to be free of that same fear and shame about their sexuality that I have experienced. I want everyone to be free to express and joyfully embrace their desires, as if they were normal, whatever those desires look like. Because they are NORMAL …at least for yourself!

Your authentic sexual desire is as distinct as your fingerprints and as natural as your eye color. You WERE born this way!

Those fears and shames about our sexuality we almost all carry, were imbedded in us by the culture, religion or family we were raised in, most of whom had not the slightest fucking clue about their own sexuality, let alone yours!

It has been a monumental liberation of my spirit, to live openly in my sexual truth in my personal and professional life.

I would imagine my experience as being out as a Fetishsexual can only be compared to someone who is gay or lesbian, who has fully come out of the closet, and is living their sexual/personal lifestyle openly.

I believe the similarity of this comparison to the gay and lesbian community is deeper than that aspect alone. I would propose that up to 15%, or more, of the human gene pool is Fetish sex driven, or as I term it, Fetishsexual. In other words, their sexual orientation is Fetish, just as 8-10% is Gay or Lesbian. This is one of the areas of psychological research I am pursuing.

How blessed I am that I get to be all of who I am in my everyday life and also specialize in researching, mapping and defining the mythic, archetypal, psychological nature of fetish sex. I believe this nature is inherent and embedded in both the personal and the collective archetypal unconscious. I am grateful these early maps have proven helpful to my clients and others seeking to feel empowered and healed in expressing their kink desires in a conscious, healthy manner.

I am celebrating that I am still on the mission I began back in 2000, with the publication of "The Sharp Edge of Love," "to raise sexuality to its rightful place alongside intellect, creativity, emotion and spirit, as a major, valid and integral aspect of the human persona."

I put this quote from myself, on the back cover of the original print version of TSEL. I am proud to say I have dedicatedly pursued that mission!

I continue to advocate for the rights of everyone to be sexually enlivened beings, expressing fully their authentic sexuality, as perverse, twisted, decadent or bizarre that may be. To be clear, my blessing assumes your sexual expression is negotiated, consensual, risk aware, legal, adult behavior.

I have been trekking out in the darker edges of human sexuality for quite some time now, and I can assure you, after many years as a 24/7 Fetish sex explorer, and Erotic Wilderness Guide, it is all and more it is hyped up to be!

And it is still a wilderness area to most. It is an unconscious wilderness, often beyond personal and public acknowledgement. But that is quickly changing.

The emergence, or better, explosion of sexuality in this current era, in all its vast variety, is entirely unprecedented in the history of civilization. This emergence is still, in most ways, very raw, immature, irresponsible, adolescent and uninformed.

The shadows of our sexuality still lead the way unfortunately at this early stage. Lying, sneaking, irresponsibility, and deceit are still a prevalent experience. Unconscious shadowy pathways that violate or circumvent consent are still being chosen over, clearly negotiated, honest, informed consent.

But this is the beginning of a new era of sexual expression and honesty. If you are reading this, I would consider you in the vanguard of those wanting to bring their sexual desire into conscious expression in the everyday norms of their life.

I want to honor that you are moving past what has held you back, maybe for decades, to at least crack the door open and peer inside. It takes tremendous courage and strength to overcome the obstacles that hold us back from our innate sexual expression.

I want to encourage you, right here, right now, to joyously embrace your sexual truths from sacred to profane, and do your best to learn and choose healthy, conscious practices in pursuing all of your desires. To fully express and explore whatever shades of sexuality you have been blessed with, it is imperative that you choose to be in integrity with yourself and others in your world.

It is the noblest of journeys!

FEAR OF YOUR SEX CREATURE

To the greatest extent human sexuality has been shrouded in fear since the dawn of civilization. Even in this era, our sexual desires, no matter their truth, are expected to be limited to the narrow confines allowed by the sex-negative cultural, family and religious mythos we are immersed in. Those who sway can expect to be punished or condemned on some level or another.

In such a morally threatening atmosphere, we often do not feel safe to be who we really are sexually. As a culture, we tend to keep our true sexual nature hidden, out of the light. But Eros is a fierce resilient creature. Even without light, it can still grow ferociously in the dark. As a result our hidden erotic yearnings are often acted out in shadowy, secretive, unhealthy, harmful ways. This secrecy just drives our personal sexual desire further into shame and fear, rather than being looked at and understood, if not welcomed and enjoyed.

This lifelong fear of our Eros coats and rigidifies the body as well as our emotions and psyches. It constricts and inhibits the instinctive physical, vocal and emotional gestures of our desire. Our movements into our authentic Erotic expression can be awkward and clumsy, our Erotic voice clenches in the throat. We can't meet the gaze of our partner. In the most extreme edges of Erotic fear, we can't get hard or wet.

Everyone wants to have great sex. Unfortunately, few do. To do so one has to venture beyond the narrow range the embedded cultural mythos deems sexually acceptable, and in some cases prohibits by law, civil or divine. Most of us keep our more primitive sexual creatures hidden and chained within the pruned, well-manicured, sterile landscape of the general culture. We are inhibited through fear and threat from venturing into the untamed, dangerous wilderness of our Eros.

What are the unconscious, but potent fears that keep people's authentic desires chained within the narrow sexual range that culture, religion and family dictate as "normal"? Since they are operating below the surface of awareness, we often overlook how much influence these fears have on what we approach or avoid sexually. They can be subtle but potent influences in determining how open or closed we are to our own desires. Unless they are resolved and brought to awareness, these unconscious fears can have a strong influence.

A potent but typical fear that holds people back from being honest about their sexuality is judgment by others. What if my partner, boss, pastor, co-workers, parents or children knew what my true desire looks like? Would I get fired, ostracized, condemned, shamed, or vilified?

Another lingering internalized belief for those with religious upbringings is that our sexual desire, outside procreation is evil, the path to hell and the devil. The temptation of a few moments pleasure could lead to eternal punishment and disgrace. Under the burden of this undercurrent of damnation, we may feel completely conflicted about the morality of our sexuality.

This fear driven aspect of our unconscious serves as the place where this repression inclines people to sneak and hide their sexual truth. Alternatively they may project all their own sordid, perverse, decadence onto others, and deny any in themselves. "Sick people do that, not me. Satan (or some other evil spirit) has devoured their weak soul. I am a good girl or boy and would never do such a horrible thing. Or, inversely my desires are sick, or I must be sick."

Many adults may have been emotionally or physically traumatized in phases of their childhood and sexual development. This adds more complexity, in some cases overwhelming complexity to embracing ones authentic sexual nature.

Unconsciously many people fear they may not be worthy, or attractive, or sexy enough. They will make a fool of themselves, or be met with rejection or embarrassment.

The good news is none of these subtle messages are valid. Each individual soul is quite worthy, attractive and sexy. Each individual has the birthright to be exactly who they are sexually and in all ways.

But these internal messages, often fortified by real life traumas and threats in our developmental years, can still hold the power to dominate and fend off our desire. To confront these self-sabotaging parts of ourselves, we have no choice but to engage and bring them more clearly into conscious awareness. One can also learn practices on how to connect with the truth that is in our bodies and souls, versus the tirelessly judgmental and inaccurate stories in our heads.

This wilderness of Eros I have spoken of is within you. Many have left their Erotic wilderness unexplored for decades, and some have abandoned their sexuality completely. It feels safer to shun sex altogether. Nonetheless your sexual desires will relentlessly and seductively beckon you to explore.

To go from the uninitiated, adolescent state of Eros most of us are trapped in to an unencumbered authentic expression of our sexuality, free of shame and exultant in our expression, can be a complex task.

It means lifting the hood and looking within at the conscious and unconscious aspects of our present state of sexual expression. We will need to look more deeply at exactly who we are sexually. This means to flesh out and allow the sexual personas that are alive within us to have more freedom to express. It means to look at all the unconscious blocks and sex-negative prohibitions imbedded in us since we were young children.

These unconscious, prohibitive messages have substantial power over our choices. You know that, if you have been stopped at the threshold of your desire, peering in longingly, but frozen in place, or have crossed into the territory and then ran back fearfully.

This book is designed to help you gain insight into the many compelling territories of Eros available to explore within yourself. It is intended to help you understand and reveal the rich, symbolic, archetypal dimensions of Eros, operating and held within your unconscious. It is about helping you prepare for your own exploration. We cannot fully know who we are Erotically, without trekking out into the territory. This book is a call to embrace your power to choose to be true to who you are as a sexual being, in a conscious, honest, mature way. This can be a tough, complex battle for many of us. And if the complexities you might encounter are misunderstood, or not accounted for, even tougher.

The tools and practices offered here are also useful for healing the shame and fear embedded in us. They support your right to choose your own pathways and begin exploring at a safe pace that fits your risk/reward thresholds.

I will cover some information about the spiritual or sacred-sex pathways of Eros. Particularly aspects that have to do with techniques to get "present", deeper into the body, and resolving the abundance of toxic shame, fear and betrayal our culture and those around us bestowed on our vulnerable, impressionable sexual psyche, as we grew up.

But my main focus, or forte, if you will, is to map out the territory of Fetish, Kink and D/s-BDSM. I feel at this stage, this is the most confusing, maligned, feared, and judged aspect of our sexual persona(s), as well as the most compelling, fascinating and liberating dimension of Erotic expression.

My own journey has immersed me in a vibrant tapestry of psychological, Erotic and personally sacred experience. Not all of these experiences have been so lofty and uplifting, particularly right at the start. My own journey began disastrously with just one step into my Erotic wilderness. I was maliciously outed by my ex, to family, friends, co-workers, my two teen sons and any stranger who would listen during our divorce. She put the most horrid spin possible on my authentic desires. I was falsely portrayed as a sick disgusting pathological pervert, unfit to be a father, husband or friend. Overnight, I became an outcast in my community, vilified and abandoned.

Except for one best friend, all the friends and people I knew over the 27 years living in my city, would not come anywhere near me nor even just ask what these wild accusations were about. I was divorcing after 17 years of stifling incompatibility and contentiousness. My leaving the marriage had nothing to do with who I was sexually. But my sexual desires around Dominance and submission and BDSM, once discovered, became the whole issue, and the "evidence" against me in my divorce.

As a result, in both the moral, social and legal court, I lost all rights to be treated fairly. I lost my home, my business, custody rights to my 2 sons, all my friends, professional associates, and a great deal of dignity. My ex told my sons I was a loser and would wind up dead in a gutter. She scared them into not having any contact with "the creep who ruined their lives." It took over a year of delicate effort to get them to see me again. There were times I genuinely feared the accuracy of her horrible prediction. It was the most devastating emotional and spiritual ruin I could have imagined.

But as well, there were unimagined blessings hidden in this seeming devastation that I am eternally grateful for. I was now free to be honest about my sexuality, without regard to anyone knowing or not. Anyone I would have wanted to hide it from now knew – even my 13 and 15-year-old sons! Without having been outed I would have never stepped into the public eye as an advocate for sexual honesty, empowerment and healing. I would have not gotten to enjoy the soulfully enriching experience of being fully true to myself and supporting others to do the same. And most importantly, I would not have been able to restore my relationship with my amazing sons over these years from this new place of honesty and authenticity.

Whatever I went through was worth getting to where I am. I will cover more detail about how to more reasonably cross this threshold in your own life in a later chapter.

If you seek to explore the depth of your own Eros, it will be impossible to approach it without also looking at all that lurks beneath the surface of your desire. All that has been tangled up with your sexuality, the parts of you that may hold you back, and the parts that are pushing you forward, will need to be differentiated and understood. Fortunately, you are not alone in this complex but rewarding endeavor.

In the privacy allowed by the Internet, many others are now drawn to the gateway of their own Erotic depths. This gateway marks the edge of the psychosexual wilderness where culturally, Eros has been exiled for millennium. This wilderness has been the forbidden zone. All that the general culture, or our own internal moral critic considers taboo, perverse, sick, evil, psycho or new-age wacky is projected onto the wilderness of Eros. All the boogey men and women of our sexually terrified cultural nightmares must certainly be out there, waiting to destroy our purity or social acceptability. This fear-driven mythos of our sexuality has left this vast Erotic wilderness mostly unexplored by both individuals and cultures – until this emerging era!

Over the last 60 plus years, people in small urban communities began to emerge to demand the freedom and fundamental right to be who they are in all ways, including sexually. The vanguard of this movement of course was the gay-rights activism that began in the late 50's. What became the prominent LGBT movement of our times, evolved from small, chaotic, angry protests over outlandish local discrimination, into a highly organized, politically savvy, activist movement tackling the broader issues of same-sex marriage, adoption rights, repeal of sodomy and other arcane, sex-related laws. They created a wide array of social, political and health networks to support their communities.

New sexual liberation movements in this current era are seeking the same acceptance and freedom to express. Numerous new sexual identities and orientations are emerging from the sexual wilderness, brought back by early pioneers, adventurers, erotic free-spirits and spiritual seekers willing to risk exploring and discovering what is true for them Erotically. More and more frequently, in this new era of sexual liberation, these sex pioneers are willing to stand up publicly and speak for their rights and the rights of others to be true to who they are.

The work ahead to establish and insure the right of all people to be free, if not encouraged, to express their personal sexuality will need to be as significant in scope and scale as the road the LGBT rights movement has gone down. The conservative, fundamentalist, institutional, sex-negative forces are mounting a strong, if not coercive counterattack against these new movements and are preparing a "War on Sex" (see Marty Klein's book) to rival the morality driven, and misguided war on drugs.

One prominent sexual identity emerging is the Fetish, Kink, or D/s-BDSM sexualities and lifestyles. Fetishsexuality as I classify it, represents a broad range of diverse practices, relationships and communities within this over-arching term. All of these various communities within this particular sexual path are pushing valiantly into this newly opened frontier of the Erotic wilderness.

On the whole, those who are striving for their sexually authentic expression within this realm, intend their activities to be conducted in a mature, consensual, risk-aware manner. In essence, Fetishsexuals are simply sexual beings seeking to experience the full ecstasy of their edgy but authentic desires with a consenting partner(s) in ways that are empowering and ecstatic to both.

Another major wave emerging over the last few decades is "spiritually" oriented Eros, commonly called sacred-sexuality in contemporary terms. These approaches to sexuality derived from such ancient traditions as Taoism, Tantra, and Quodoshka. These practices are intended to cultivate your sexuality or sexual energy as a path of enlightenment, awareness and open-heartedness. This book will not focus on this path specifically, but will draw in many valuable tools and practices from these arts that create greater presence, mindfulness, embodiment, healing and compassionate communication between partners.

Polyamory is also significant emerging trend. According to Wikipedia, Polyamory "is the practice, desire, or acceptance of intimate relationships that are not exclusive with respect to other sexual or intimate relationships, with knowledge and **consent** of everyone involved. "

Polyamory, often abbreviated as *Poly*, is often described as "consensual, ethical, and responsible **non-monogamy**". The word is sometimes used in a broader sense to refer to sexual or romantic relationships that are not sexually exclusive, though there is disagreement on how broadly it applies; an emphasis on ethics, honesty, and transparency all around is widely regarded as the crucial defining characteristic."

These and other emerging sexual identities and expressions including trans, queer, asexual, eco-sexual and more are still recent outposts gaining a foothold in the wilderness of Eros. They are like primitive settlements merely a few days trek into the wilds by foot, past the edge of mainstream sexual civilization. The rest of the wilderness lies well beyond these early out posts, like a vast Amazon Jungle of Erotic riches and also certain dangers, as uncharted territory always is.

Because of my own traumatic experience in attempting to live authentically in my sexual truth, it has brought me to a strong place of compassion and advocacy for sexual freedom and tolerance and the right of everyone to express their sexual truth. If I can support others on this journey, to move beyond the fear holding them back and embrace and express their sexuality, I am grateful to do so.

Sex is Friction – Eros is Myth

In the sex-negative, sex-ignorant culture we are immersed in, it may never have occurred to you that there is more to consider and explore beyond the friction-level sex most of us have engaged in. Friction level sex, while often quite satisfying, is of generally short duration. It just dusts the surface of the Erotic depths we are capable of experiencing, and are instinctively inclined to desire.

It's reported that the average man, when engaging his sexual partner, ejaculates in about seven minutes …or less! Men, listen up—anything under a half hour should be considered premature ejaculation!

That is of course meant to be a provocative statement, not a judgment on men. In fairness, the invitation here is aimed at both men and women to explore further into their dance of Eros. Less than a half hour of lovemaking may mean missing the deeper realms of erotic ecstasy waiting for you both, just over the horizon of friction sex.

Finding your way to these deeper realms has something to do of course with not relying solely on friction, or intense friction while engaging sexually. In these realms of Eros the mission is not ejaculation or orgasm per se, but immersion in the ecstatic, intimate, body, spirit and soul experience of the vast Erotic landscape. The potency is in the ecstasy of the shared journey itself, not only in the destination.

For men who are literally challenged by premature ejaculation, what follows can offer insights into engaging your sexual expression more enduringly and confidently.

Think of the most compelling, wise, enlivening, or romantic book, play or movie you have been inspired by. Not getting past the friction realm of sex is like only going a few pages or minutes into these epic tales…and stopping there…over and over and over again. You will never get to experience the full scope of these great works of art, or the depths of your and your partner's Eros, if you never take the time to have the full experience they are designed to inspire in you.

So what is the difference between sex as friction versus an Erotic dance? Friction sex, to the greatest extent, has been classically summarized as slam, bam and thank you...though there may not be a lot to be thankful for, at least from your partner's point of view, but likely from yours as well.

Friction sex can be a great relief, generate connection, and shake one loose from frustration or horniness for a brief time. The outcome can be cathartic. It can even be fantastic. Orgasms just feel great period! But look back over your shoulder for a moment, at that relentless, fierce, passionate drive that led to friction sex.

You might start to see that part of you, the core of your desire, was all geared up to take this epic journey to the farthest reaches of Eros, and you just got off, literally, at the first exit you came to, a few miles down the highway. Again, not knocking friction sex, solo or other. When highly sexed people are busy, a quick excursion into release can smooth out the rough edges of the day and satisfy your inner sex-creature hunger. But this is just dusting the surface of deep, and little understood dimensions of human sexuality.

Unfortunately, as a culture, we lack or prohibit even the most basic sex-education, let alone offer insight into the ecstatic realms of Eros. Fortunately for all of us, we are just entering the era where sexuality pioneers have been opening new vistas of our vast Erotic potential. Word of these practices, activities and insights are proliferating on the Internet, and being offered in books, and workshops or personal guidance by an array of skilled, innovative practitioners. They are opening the gateways to allow human sexuality to flow like water, beyond the reach of mainstream obstructions.

There are two main pathways coming into view, leading into the farther realms of Eros. In many ways, they are polar opposites of each other. One is popularly called Sacred Sexuality, the other Fetish sexuality. Each can be personally meaningful, combined together or be pursued separately. The nature of these two poles of sexual expression - spiritual/soulful, sacred/profane, or refined/wild are what I consider the yin/yang of Eros. Both poles offer important considerations to clarify, in order to begin conscious, negotiated, consensual engagement of the deeper aspects of your personal Eros. Normal in all cases is personal to you, not what the mainstream political, psychological or religious view dictates, nor your current partner(s) for that matter.

For a good number of people, their deepest yearning may be to engage in the Eros of heart centered, lovemaking. The energy is tender, sweet, compassionate, romantic. Some seek to cultivate this energy further towards an ecstatic, out of body explosion of bliss and connection.

This is towards the Spiritual path or sacred notions of sex that are re-emerging in this era. The drive of Eros in this direction is an ascent. The pleasures are refined. The ultimate intention is to transmute sexual energy from the root of the sex organs through the body to the crown of the head. This encourages one to journey out of the body, rise above personal desire and identity, aspire to the heavens, and merge with some sense of divine ecstatic universal consciousness.

This path of sacred sexuality is often called in contemporary terms neo-Tantra. It includes practices of breath-work, ejaculation control or orgasm cycling, meditations and yoga postures drawn from ancient traditions such as Tantra, Taoism, and others. These can involve rigorous disciplines and devotion to techniques to shift one's awareness towards spiritual enlightenment from the mundane or profane pleasures or entanglements of the lower realms. The rigor involved in such practices may be well-beyond most people's intention or desire.

Nonetheless, these ancient Erotic arts do offer many practical techniques that are easy to learn and use to expand awareness, presence, embodiment, intention, deep-listening/observation and other valuable skills important along any sexual path. These can be essential practices to open to your and your partner's Erotic potentials in any direction you may journey. They help ground your exploration in intention, communication, trust, heart-to-heart intimacy, physical connection, and emotional/physical safety.

The other major direction on the path of Eros is what I will call the Soulful path. This path of Eros is personal versus universal, primitive more than refined. This path of Eros is a descent, deeper down into the body, earthbound, pulsating, into the wild, instinctual aspects of our being. These are often considered the taboo, forbidden realms of Eros by the culture at large, inhabited by dark, dangerous but alluring sexual figures. This is dropping down into the very personal realms of our sexual identity and into the unpruned wilds of Eros.

These roots of our wildest sexual desires extend far into our evolutionary heritage of mammalian alpha/beta pecking order instincts, and deeper into predator/prey reptilian level instincts. They include the unconscious instinctual psychologies and physical symbolic communication gestures still programmed into the modern human psyche. These encompass aspects of our sexual expression related to power exchange, hot-blooded dominance and submission and cold-blooded sadist/masochist expressions.

This is the realm of Fetishsexuality. Here we find a rich archetypal symbolic mythos at play, with stories, plots and characters ranging across a pantheon of paired personas such as Mommy/son, Daddy/daughter, Teacher/student, Master or Mistress/slave and many more in some sort of power exchange. These pairings of two or more may be further differentiated through an array of emerging gender and sexual identities.

These mythic, often unconscious structures of our Erotic desire find their way to the surface through our fantasies when we engage sexually, where they can drive one to orgasm or other deep erotic states. When engaged consciously and allowed to express and embody authentically with a consenting partner, these fierce explorations of our dark, wild instinctual edges can offer a profound sense of empowerment and acceptance, as well as a full-body, soulful, exquisitely spent bliss from either side of the power exchange.

If you have been living in the realm of friction sex only, then the bulk of your Erotic expression may still be beyond your conscious gaze. But if you have sensed a depth of hidden erotic expression yet untapped then I encourage you to begin to explore this potential within you.

Maybe you already have a very specific sense, or have even explored what your deeper Eros looks like, if it was allowed to roam freely. For others, it may require some effort to untangle your authentic and ecstatic Erotic yearnings from all that has resisted them. This may include drilling down below the decades of shame, fear, guilt, secrecy or denial your authentic sexual desires may have been buried under.

To discover and learn more about these erotic pathways from either direction, sacred or profane, there are plenty of websites, books, workshops and guides around for support for you and/or your partner's exploration.

Either path, from Sacred Sex to Fetish Sex is clearly more complex, nuanced and subjective than friction sex, so the more you educate yourself the more fulfilling your explorations can become. While external resources can be very helpful, ultimately it is about finding and cultivating your own personally meaningful expression.

For either path, it is critical that both partners follow and agree on certain ethical codes to build the trust required to reach the most potent depths of your desires.

This means to have an intention and commitment to being in integrity, being responsible, accountable, risk-aware, actively listening and being present. It means telling the truth, starting with what you want…and what you don't. Impeccable respect of boundaries is critical. Clear, transparent and fair negotiation with your partners is standard procedure. Knowing proper techniques and risk/safety factors for your style of engagement and the toys or tools involved, goes without saying. Encouragement and compassionate support of your partner is a golden practice.

Adhering to these practices and principles builds the foundations of trust, safety and mutual care for an ongoing and deepening exploration. This framework offers the possibility of engaging and sharing our most protected and vulnerable Erotic depths with our partners.

While this can seem a complex effort overall, the fundamentals of consciously engaging and exploring your Eros are easy to develop and learn as a practice. Here are some core tips. I will elaborate on these in more detail in subsequent chapters.

1. Personal Embodiment

The place to begin is your own body.

We as a culture and men in particular have become considerably disembodied. We live from the neck up, in rational analysis, in stories in our head, in judgments about others and ourselves. We live in a thought-stream of anxiety about the future and regret about the past. We are often barely aware that we have a body and exist within it in this moment right now. You can be a hardcore workout geek, runner and intensely athletic but still not be consciously aware of your body.

When we are not consciously embodied, we are unconsciously embodied. This unconscious embodiment displays in some subtle to overt fashion, the ways we are shut down, afraid, disconnected, in shame, lack confidence and numerous other physical expressions of our inner feelings in a given moment.

So start with your own body awareness and begin getting in touch with these subtler layers of yourself! This means cultivating practices to get out of your head and deeper into the body. This can be conscious movement, breath-work, yoga, tai-chi and other such practices. These can help you drop down into awareness of your body, and reach clarity of what you desire right now, or what resists your desire.

2. Presence and Intention

These practices are gateways to learning presence, the art of being fully engaged, aware and embodied right here, right now. This state of presence is the place to form the intention you have set for the current moment or engagement. Having a conscious intention, especially for sexual exploration, is a powerful anchor point to return to, anytime you're busy anxious mind may distract you.

3. Ambiance

There is also the setting and ambiance for your Erotic journey to consider. In ritual language this is called preparing the "container" or sacred space to hold the experience in. The container is both symbolic and physical. It divides reality into an outer realm of your everyday life and inner realm or container that holds what you want to focus on in the moment. In practical terms this container can be a dedicated space in your dwelling that you establish for ongoing use, or one created for the moment if your current living situation does not allow a permanent space.

In this setting that will hold your Erotic journey, you can create the ambiance that best supports the intended experience. Choose the lighting, soundscape, colors, aromas, textures and more that enlivens you, soothes you, excites you. Same for the attire you choose. These are the personal touches that create comfort, ease, empowerment and safety for the experience. Ambiance is sensorial. It supports you being deeper in your body through sensory activations of the nervous system that "turn" your body on. This naturally enhances your sense of presence and embodiment. We do many of these practices instinctively in our homes on date nights, and doing so consciously can really enhance the potency of your container.

4. Mutual Embodiment

It can be very helpful to begin Erotic engagement between new or established partners, with non-erotic physical connection. This can include doing conscious breath and movement practices together with your partner or mutual massage. The body has an amazing capacity to shed tension, especially surface tension. Surface tensions are physical reflections of those mildly nagging judgments, distractions or anxieties, and other mind chatter, that are not really relevant to the intention of this present moment. Letting your bodies simply interact together will allow the natural intimacy and connection you share with your partner to blossom forth and allow desire to flow unimpeded.

5. Clear Negotiation

Prior to any sexual engagement, negotiate clearly with your partner for the journey into Eros you wish to undertake together. Get clear about specific desires for the engagement you want to explore, get clear about boundaries around areas that are not desired or are to be prohibited. Get clear about safe-words or other means to halt the Erotic journey if something comes up that was not in the original negotiation. Get clear about safe-sex practices and sexual histories needed to protect you both. I recommend always checking in at the beginning of each engagement, even with a long-term partner, to clarify past agreements, and review any new physical or emotional data that may be calling for modifying previously agreed upon activities.

Your partner has likely been immersed in the same sex-negative shames, fears, mistrust or actual traumas around their natural sexual expression as you may have. Their disconnection from their Erotic core and its full embodiment may be well beyond your own, or vice-versa. There can be numerous factors involved that subtly want to resist deeply engaging one's Eros, even between long-term partners.

Being thorough and conscientious with the above considerations, safeguards, intimacies and communications can go a long way in breaking through many long-held layers of unconscious resistance that run counter to one's stated and sincere desires.

Be clear, direct, and thorough in your negotiation, both partners with full equality, voice, and advocacy. I highly discourage ever engaging in Kink or any alternative sexual engagement with someone you just hooked-up with online, in the bar or even your own on-going partner if you have not already come to a complete agreement on all fronts of engagement.

The potential for perceived or actual consent violations, mis-understandings, resentment, mistrust or emotional or physical harm are excessive when there has not been a clear negotiation. The point is to feel empowered, connected and exhilarated after engaging your deepest desires, not wounded.

Start the negotiation with an intention to make a heart-felt, human-to-human connection before you enter into any level of D/s-BDSM, even if this will be a casual or one time connection. The foundation for exploring these powerful depths of our sexual desires is trust. Each side needs to know they are safe and ultimately cared for while revealing and expressing vulnerable and often scary parts of their sexual desire. Maintain self-advocacy as your funda-mental responsibility and right. If you are not fully ready, or some-thing does not feel right then exercise your right to disengage or slow the pace down before you do choose to engage.

Conduct your negotiation in as honest, transparent and reveal-ing a manner as possible. This is critical. Be clear about intention. It is important to clarify your intentions, boundaries and expectations during and also beyond the initial encounter. If you want to enter the encounter with no expectations afterward, state that clearly right up front. Make sure your potential partner understands your inten-tion. Press for a direct response that they understand and agree. If you do not wish to engage without there being some sense that you are both considering a relationship or connection beyond this one engagement, be clear about that. Hold your boundaries firmly if a potential partner says they are looking for casual only, and you seek more, and vice versa.

Discuss clearly what may be involved in an initial engagement with your partner in terms of props, toys, roles and intensities. Get clear about safe sex practices to maintain, and sexual history.

Start slow and keep it simple if you are just beginning. Get clarity about options for what to do if something unexpected comes up during the engagement. This would include usage and agreement on safe-words.

Some issues that may arise as you engage may just need you to pause and check in with each other, and then continue. Others may require you to come to a complete stop, and check in about what has come up and what one or the other needs most in that moment. Sometimes, even with clear negotiations, there are things that can present unexpectedly.

The best thing to do in these situations is to pause, breathe, stay calm, ask, listen and shift your presence to full compassion and care for the partner needing support. These occurrences will likely be rare if ever, with proper preparation. But by considering them in the initial negotiation, the trust this builds will actually reduce even further the likelihood of unanticipated interruptions. If you start with a simple engagement plan, and move forward at a reasonable pace, you can have a compelling, intimate and deeply erotic journey with your partner, even if it is your first engagement.

Even for a novice, a wide range of play and toys can be explored with a common sense level of safety, communication and pace. These could include spanking by hand or various paddles, wearing wrist or ankle cuffs, non-choking collars, blindfolds, or various insertibles for example. More intense forms of play, such as full rope bondage, suspension, needle play, or single tails, usually identified as edge play, should require taking a class, workshop or intensive practice to insure safety and well-being all around. All of the aspects I am referring to can be researched online to help give you a broader understanding or answer questions you might have about specific forms of Kink.

6. Dance Together

Once you begin to move into your Erotic expression, stay in awareness of your connection to your partner. I look at it like a very intimate dance like the tango. The connection is palpable. Both move freely in their own intricacy, yet they move as one, with no break in the connection.

Pace is also very important, particularly in the Fetish explorations where there is a desire for intense physical, psychological and emotional engagement. Slow pace is best to start with. It helps you adjust and shift more readily to where the flow may want to go in the moment. Stay aware of your partner's breath, tone of voice, posture, skin tone. If you feel or sense some measure of disconnect or loss of flow, use these cues to get present with what it is your partner may be signaling. Do this for yourself as well.

Reading the body is equivalent to reading the mind. The body is the analog of and mirrors the unconscious. It reflects what is being said in the unspoken dimensions of communication. This can be very important if your partner is challenged or wounded around their body, desirability or carries sexual shame. Staying connected, encouraging, present and safe will create trust and support them to remain in the ecstasy of the dance. If uncertain of what the signals may mean, stop and check in with your partner directly.

7. Afterglow

Plan for and take time immediately after your Erotic journey to let yourselves linger in the afterglow of your shared experience. Aftercare for you both can be as important to you both as the initial negotiation. Linger together in this altered state of physical and emotional intimacy. Bask in the glow of erotic intensity. Take it nice and slow. Cuddle, breathe together, lay quiet, connected, aware and in appreciation of yourself and your partner.

These desires we can experience together are intoxicating and compelling enough to sweep us down into an exquisite pool of taboo sexual ecstasies. Staying present and embodied in this at-ease state can help deepen your sense of how natural your authentic sexual expression is.

Embrace your partner in ways that signal your care, appreciation and love for who they are and what you were able to share together. Enjoy and surrender to the profound, blissful stillness that may be present.

Be aware there can be a tendency for some to drop back into old patterns of shame, unworthiness, judgments, and other woundings, almost instantly. Staying physically connected, remembering to breath, feeling gratitude and staying present with your partner can help ground your authentic Erotic beings as the natural, integral and welcome aspect of your psyches they are meant to be.

Having crossed the threshold of our edgiest sexual desires does not necessarily mean we have now transcended or healed all the ways we may have been previously hiding, fearing or in shame about our desires.

We have all been immersed in and have internalized, to one degree or another, this highly toxic, sex-negative, shaming culture. It can be quite possible that these deeply internalized, judgmental parts many of us may have, will attempt to wage an assault on your vulnerable psyche after you have indulged your desire. For some this can happen soon after the scene, or in the days that follow.

Prepare in advance for this situation by a good aftercare plan that includes access to emotional support if needed in the days following or sooner if needed. This can be as simple as sharing with your partner about any of your feelings, or just being held and breathing together. This care applies to the Dominant and submissive both. Moving deeper into your authentic sexual desires is an opportunity for both to be empowered and to heal.

It can be helpful to allow some time in the days ahead to debrief and reflect about the experience each had. This allows you both to learn more about the other and make key adjustments to enhance the Erotic excursions ahead.

There is never any end to the pleasures, passions, and intimacy Eros offers when engaged in with care, integrity and awareness. Journey well into this empowering, ecstatic and enlivening experience!

HOW TO WELCOME YOUR SEX CREATURE
5 KEYS TO BEING SEXUALLY AUTHENTIC, CONSCIOUS, AND EMPOWERED

Being sexually authentic is your birthright. Sharing your deepest sexual truths with a trusted partner is one of the most loving, liberating, intimate and ecstatic of human experiences.

Many men and women hide authentic aspects of their sexual desire...for good reason! Our sex-negative culture, family, religions and even our relationships often deny us a safe, welcoming place to honor and discuss the full spectrum of our sexual desires. They seldom honor, bless and respect any but the narrowest view of acceptable sexual practice or frequency. In fact, the tangible fear of being shamed, harshly judged, or of losing relationships, family or friends can leave many choosing to stay secretive or shadowy about their true sexual desire. Some people are so deep in shame and guilt they can't get past the fear of speaking openly about their desires to those closest to them. Some can become consumed by fantasy, masturbation or porn rather than risk openly expressing what's true to their partners...or even to themselves.

Many people were emotionally wounded (shamed or terrorized) as boys and girls around their sexuality, if not in fact sexually abused. Many may have developed shyness or embarrassment, loss of trust, loss of confidence. They may have internalized the harsh voice of sex-negative moral judgment from their father or mother, religion or culture into their inner dialogue, or project that onto others. And to one extent or another, if they are secretive in their sexual expressions as adults, they carry an innate fear of being discovered at the wrong time or place, the feeling of being busted, the fall from grace and the consequences that might bring.

Getting honest about our sexual desires can be a struggle, even in a supportive environment. To become sexually whole, it is important to learn and practice techniques to consciously engage and embrace your authentic desires, and share them honestly in a healthy, fulfilling, consensual manner. This is also the path to begin to resolve the conflicted, wounded, shadowy, dis-empowered aspects of your sexuality.

Most people have a complex authentic sexual persona, as distinct as a fingerprint and inherent as their eye-color, whether they are consciously aware of it or not. There can be light aspects and shadow aspects, the parts we show and the parts we hide. There can be tender sweet aspects and primitive, wild instinctual aspects. These sharp contrasts do not necessarily cancel each other, but are a paradox that one can learn to hold honorably and in an ecstatically potent way sexually. Both light and shadow aspects of our sexuality possess a pantheon of archetypal parts and counterparts that we may carry at an unconscious level.

These sexual personas, or sex creatures as I sometimes call them, are distinct and independent from our outer social personas. They are typical and prevalent in the emerging Kink oriented sexual orientations. Examples of these embedded sexual archetypes can be dominant/submissive, predator/prey, beast/beauty, bad boy/good girl, rapist/victim, teacher/student, mommy-daddy/son-daughter, older man-woman/younger man-woman to name just a few. All and any of these expressions of Eros can be valid and authentic. They are far more typical within the sexual landscape than many want to believe. But for those so inclined, it is just their personal sexual baseline. It is their normal!

Finding safe ways to express these sexual energies consciously and consensually can be powerful, healing and ecstatically fulfilling. A hallmark of practicing conscious engagement of your sexuality is that there be nothing involved that would be ultimately harmful or non-consensual in your engagement with partners. Being consciously sexual means to encourage whatever is true in the realm of your fantasy to express with as little inhibiting judgment, shame or fear as possible. Being consciously sexual supports a safe, consensual exploration to occur. Clearly negotiated consent and other conscious practices can support the expression of any sexual desire, no matter how taboo.

I want to encourage you to raise your authentic sexuality out of the shadows to its rightful place alongside of your intellect, emotion, creativity and spirit as an integral aspect of your personality.

I want to turn now to address some issues particular to men.

I feel there would be counter parts to what follows that could be addressed to women, but since the male side is the side I know most directly, I offer this view.

There is some percentage of men still stuck in their immature, adolescent, non-consensual, brutish if not violent expression of their sexuality. This carries over to their attitudes in their interaction to women in general.

In my opinion, this is the result of a culture that does not provide adolescent boys a contemporary process of initiation into mature masculinity. This leaves masculinity stuck in its adolescent manifestation to one degree or another throughout adulthood. This brutish masculine sensibility is also the result of an educational system that offers no responsible sex-positive sex education, no sexual diversity training, communication/negotiation skills and no discussions of sexual consent and responsibility, not to mention anything about the ecstatic mutual pleasure and intimacy sex offers.

Instead this critical stage of development for boys takes place on the playground, in the locker room and hyper-masculine athletics culture or worse, street gangs. Here the dark violence of the un-initiated shadow masculine reigns.

These omissions generate the class of men capable of rape, date rape, gang rape, sexual assault, domestic violence and other tragic manifestations of the uninitiated masculine.

As well, many men live disembodied lives. They hang in the territory of the rational analytical mind. They have no experience or guidance in how to engage a woman with presence, sensuous touch, or listening to the cues a woman's body offers that tracks the right pace of playful, loving or intense Erotic engagement.

On the other hand, many men in our culture have been socialized to keep their authentic sexuality on a leash, where it is hidden, secreted, shamed and harshly judged by the unconscious mind and culture at large. This has led to a culture of men hiding, sneaking, porning in secret, going to strip clubs, hiring prostitutes as a shadowy way to express their true desires.

And finally, there are the men who have lost their masculine edge. They are dominated into passive submission by an emasculating environment, family, community or partner. They cannot set or hold boundaries, speak up for themselves with passion, or push back when shoved…or not until their unresolved anger, shame or fear blows up in a triggered shadow driven explosion.

If you are a man who has not yet taken on whatever personal inner work that may be holding you back from the conscious expression of your sexuality, it is time to get to work! Do all you can to learn about being more embodied, present, transparent, vulnerable, passionate, powerful and all the aspects of your beautiful masculine soul that are in your court. One organization that supports men in these regards is The Mankind Project. MKP has centers all over the world that hold trainings and create ongoing connections between men seeking to get into integrity and reclaim their authentic masculine dignity and strength. I have been personally involved for almost two decades and what I have learned about myself and my shadows has been most important to my life and work. You can check them out at *The Mankind Project*.

If your intention is to be an honorable and conscious man, your authentic sexuality does not deserve to be vilified, unloved, hidden and scorned. Welcome it out of the wasteland of your unconscious that entangles it with all the despicable shaming judgments placed on it – sex-addict, deviant, disgusting, creepy selfish, rapist and every dark projection imaginable. You have every right to embrace, honor, bless, love and advocate for your sexual right to be exactly, unapologetically who you are.

For both men and women, I encourage you to hold your sexuality up to the light and cheer! Know that somewhere out there in the gene pool are plenty of cohorts who will respect and admire your sexual honesty, if not be ecstatically turned-on by your desire. Start there. Claim what is yours. Start to bring your personal sexual truth into your own aware, benevolent acknowledgment.

My intention for everyone is to stimulate your own natural yearning to be fully sexually authentic. Now is the perfect time to begin your own inquiry into the deepest realms of your sexuality.

For me this has meant developing viewpoints and practices that encourage clients to express whatever their authentic desire is and untangle and diminish whatever resists, judges or fears the conscious expression of their desire. From my work with many clients over the years, I have developed what I call the 5 Keys for consciously engaging the fullest range of your desire and find fulfillment in sex, life and relationships.

THE 5 KEYS TO EMBRACING YOUR SEXUALITY AND FINDING FULFILLMENT IN LIFE & RELATIONSHIPS
1. Sexual Authenticity

Each person has an innate, authentic sexual identity, as distinct as a fingerprint, and as inherent as your eye color. It defines how strong and frequent your natural rhythm of desire is, the erotic types you are attracted to, and the core themes your sexual desire is driven by, from sacred to profane, tender to rough, mild to wild. I define this core theme for a fetish driven sexuality as a Personal Erotic Myth. The nature of a PEM will be detailed further in subsequent chapters. Your authentic sexuality, fetish and otherwise is independent from any influence, experience, belief or trauma taken on while growing up. But often, early sex-negative influences and experiences can be tangled up with our authentic desire. These generally unresolved parts of our psyche can resist, fear, judge or make concerted efforts to inhibit, thwart or eliminate our natural desire. These are the first steps – get clear about the deeper dimensions of your sexual desire, own what your personal sexual truth is and start to untangle all that inhibits its expression.

2. Sexual Honesty

Your authentic sexuality is your birthright! Once you know what is sexually authentic for you, the next step is to learn how to express it honorably and in a forthright manner. This will mean working through all that has kept it hidden in shame, fear and harsh internal judgments, so that you can move beyond those into a place of conscious advocacy. This will be critical in order to clearly communicate what you desire and deserve sexually, and avoid disastrous erotic mismatches in your future relationships. Part of this practice will be to create a safe environment to encourage and support your partners to be honest as well, and bless them for their own sexual honesty.

3. Sexual Empowerment

By developing easy to use practices of conscious intention, negotiation skills to review and set boundaries, discussions about consent, cultivating presence, physical embodiment, and mindfulness you can learn to advocate for and embody fully your own authentic desires. These practices will also help diminish all that resists your desire physically, emotionally and psychologically. Becoming more empowered in your authentic sexuality does not mean you have resolved decades of shame, fear, harsh judgments or other serious issues that may have occurred around your sexuality. That can be a much deeper level of personal work to be undertaken.

Opening to the depths of your sexuality can be a perfect starting point to begin that deeper work. Practicing these techniques can allow you to be more aware of and have an intention or choice about whether those past issues need to be around every moment, if they do not support your sexual exploration. You can learn to put them aside and be present with your intention in the moment and who you are with right now. This level of presence itself generates tremendous trust and safety – the bedrock of any hot engagement with your partners - no matter how off the charts and edgy the desires may be. This level of awareness and intention is where you and your partner can begin to be engaged in a deep dance of intimacy and connection, and you can become an extraordinarily present, embodied, ecstatic lover to your partner(s).

4. Sexual Shadow

Sexual dishonesty is a near pandemic in our culture. We are not encouraged by the culture to be sexually honest about our true desires, so we practice sexual dishonesty by default. Our authentic sexuality does not go away through concealing it. Instead it gets pushed down into the secretive, deceptive realms below the surface, and acted out in risky if not disastrous ways. On the other hand our sexual shadow's impact may be to repress, deny, project onto others, or engage in harmful non-sexual diversions that also damage our personal well-being, and ultimately, our relationships. It is critical to bring awareness to the ways you may be expressing or hiding your sexual desires in shadowy, secretive, unhealthy ways. This is an important step in consciously embracing your authentic sexuality and learning to express it in a mature forthright manner.

5. Paradox

Learning to understand and embrace paradox allows us to accept we can be both frequent, perverse, wild, dark and taboo in our desires without detracting anything from our ability and desire to be a loving, tender, honorable, and considerate of our partners. Being authentic sexually does in no way detract from our being a good parent, partner, worker, citizen or spiritual, soulful being. The task here is to learn how to hold both your darkest desires and your most lofty aspirations for the world in an aware and noble balance that is in integrity with your agreements to your partners and yourself.

There is no perfection in all this. We will fail if we are striving for perfection. But we can develop a strong intention to honor our own personal sexual truth, and be in integrity with our agreements and values, even if we stumble at times. And we can develop practices that help us continually renew our connection to our intention to be conscious men and women sexually and otherwise.

WHAT IS AN EROTIC MYTHOS?

For many, this concept may be foreign. In a sex-negative culture, that denies the pleasures of the body and sexual fantasy, most of us have not ventured very far in exploring the unconscious story lines that may be playing out during sex with a partner, or in solitary masturbatory revelry.

I know from my own early experience, and from working with clients who had yet to uncover these inner Erotic stories, they were only glimpsed in those brief ecstatic moments right before the frenzied liberation of orgasm.

In that last minute or so before cumming, the rich truth of one's Eros, no matter how well hidden, can no longer be held back. It bursts forth and animates the body in wild, fierce gestures. It explodes from the voice in a truncated blasphemy such as..."oh god, fuck me, YES! Please, harder, deeper, slut, whore, bitch", and less decipherable, primitive grunts and screams. This is just a climactic sound byte from the full story being expressed internally.

In vanilla sex, these last moments before cumming are like unlocking a highly compacted zip file of your Personal Erotic Myth. In that moment, the story is being played out in the subconscious mind like the super speedy talk of the guy reading the disclaimers at the end of those pharmaceutical commercials or car sale ads. Only way faster!

If one were able to slow those last moments before cumming way down, and observe what is really going on, you might get a glimpse of the mythic story that drives you to orgasm. Within that packed and condensed zip file there may be a rich, compelling tale unfolding. It is a story generated and played out deep within your Erotic psyche when you have sex. Like any story, there is prologue, setting, props, attire, lead characters, dialogue, body language and action. There are mythic archetypal personas taking part in the story. Each counterpart represents a dyad drawn from a pantheon of pairs in the collective Erotic archives. Some classic pairs are Daddy/

daughter, Mommy/son, Teacher/student, Master/slave, Bad boy/ good girl, and Supreme Bitch/cuckold.

There are hundreds of variations. Someone may have a single major theme, or may be able to shift into a variety of these pairings. Often, an over-riding sense of alpha/beta Dominance and submission is at play, and in its more primitive forms, predator/prey.

This brings the unconscious instinctual aspects of our sexuality into view. These are rooted, I believe, in the pre-human psychologyical structures that are part of our biological ancestry, from the mammalian (Alpha/beta pecking orders) and reptilian (predator/ prey survival) stages of evolution. These aspects of our hard-wired psychology and behavior have been shoved way below the surface through the "civilizing" we have undergone as a species over the last several thousand years. Being civilized, cultivated, rational, refined and sophisticated is the mask we wear over our more primitive, instinctual natures.

But humans are far from civilized and the beast within runs rampant across the world, savaging families, communities, cultures, countries and the environment, as has been the operational motif of the civilized world, since civilization began. The cold-blooded reptile and the blood-thirsty, domineering, territorial mammal aspect of human nature shows up nightly in the evening news, depicting the rampant barbarism an individual, group or nation deploys on their foes and innocents alike.

These barbaric forces in the world are a reflection of the instinctive behaviors that we as individuals also attempt to civilize. But this is not entirely possible. We are not so civilized, nor capable of being so civilized, so we do the next best thing. We attempt to hide, bury, fight against, deny, repress, or project these darker aspects of who we are onto others. But as inherent aspects of our biological heritage, we cannot get rid of them. Our best efforts to ignore or repress these instinctive, wild parts of ourselves only drives them into a shadow dimension of our consciousness, where they inevitably leak out and cause havoc in our lives.

For a glimpse of how a shadow operates, think of what a closet smoker, alcoholic or drug addict goes through. The cover-up is desperately maintained, in all manner of ingenious, awkward, and avoidant ways, but getting caught is almost inevitable. A shadow is the part of us that wants to keep things hidden, desperately at times, and schemes all manner of elaborate cover-ups to maintain the image we are trying to hold up.

In the realm of sexuality, this shadow drama plays out over and over. Sexual dishonesty and cover-ups of all sorts ultimately bring destructive consequences to the individuals, relationships and families. This is pervasive at all levels of society.

To take your own sexuality out of the shadows, and begin to bring it into the light, in an honest, healthy fulfilling way, requires a deeper examination than our culture generally allows or encourages. It may involve doing inner psychological work to recover the personal agency to be sexually empowered, and examine unresolved shame, fear, sex-negative judgments or traumas about one's sexuality.

To discover and embrace your own Personal Erotic Mythos will require taking the time to look at what is happening in the condensed revelations before orgasm. It is possible to review these in depth through meditative, imaginal and ritual techniques.

For some, their erotic stories and fantasies may already be quite well developed and clear, if as yet unexpressed in real time. Many people can begin accessing these parts of themselves through writing erotica, participating in sexual fantasy chat or IM's, or journaling. Some have known exactly who they are erotically since childhood, for others it comes into view later in life. Regardless, the fantasies themselves can be very elaborate and the psychological nuances of their desires decadently compelling.

For those who do not have a sexual orientation related to a Kink driven PEM, the revelations of a Fetishsexual may appear quite shocking and even pathological. But Fetish fantasies are relatively generic from the global view. Check out sites like Fetlife, Kinkly and other Kink oriented sites and this collective pantheon of Erotic archetypal personas can be seen being woven into the personal Eros of millions of Fetishsexuals over and over again.

Individuals can learn to embrace and embody their innate variation of an Erotic archetypal ideal. Fetish driven individuals seek out partners that embrace and personalize the particular Erotic counterpart to their own. Daddy/daughter orientations, one of the most prevalent pairings in the Fetish dating and mating realms, is a prime example. Most often there is a complex variety of related themes that blends into an overall persona.

Here is an excerpt from a client who describes her dark edged desires for objectification, ownership, dehumanization and control like this. It was ultimately a gateway to a deeply felt and exhilarating freedom:

> *"I am really compelled by the feeling of being an object. A piece of property to be used and manipulated as my Master/Owner desires. The object has no voice and no need other than to serve its purpose. It's very stimulating for me to feel this type of rush, my mind literally is brain-washed. When my ass is being violated, my mind and body work in tandem...this is what my purpose is, it feels violating and it is, I am just a whore, my body is owned...it is supposed to endure and receive...be open and accepting...be surrendered. It's a degrading process to feel my asshole being stretched and then to make it relax and open...normally I would struggle and resist...but in this state of mind...I can surrender.*

> *"The dehumanized feeling...I don't want to say it turns me into a robot but it does in some ways. I guess it allows me to be "molded"...if you want a whore, then that's what I am...if you want a pain-slut...then that's what I am...if you want me to beg for abuse...then that's what I do...if you say to swallow the butt plug up my ass...then that's what I do.*

> *"It feels amazing to be free of control, to do what I am told and to be hungry and eager for it. I find the thought of clamps, weights, plugs, and degrading body-writings all do wonders at shedding my dignity. Having my hands bound also helps prevent any resistance and keeps*

me in my place. In this state, I am a whore but I'm not thinking about cumming just about being good property."

And another description from a sub male POV from the **Personal Erotic Myth Survey**:

"I am wearing a leash and naked. She is fully clothed except for her boots, which I take off one by one. She then asks me to lick her nylons or socks. She enjoys it, saying that I was doing a good job. Then she takes off her socks, and asks me to lick her toes. We are in her bedroom whilst this is going on. She is watching Dirty Dancing and enjoying my company. Finally I get a reward, to lick her pussy and her feet, to pleasure her. It is a sub's ultimate reward. I don't leave her until she is fully pleasured."

For many people though, their erotic personas are still buried, just out of conscious reach. There is awareness of a compelling desire…to be dominant or submissive, to be taken, raped, to have innocence violated, to be in total control, to be a slut, and all other variations of desire. When I ask a client about more detail of what that might look like for them, they often don't know. "I just want to be taken, told what to do," may be as much detail as they can muster. It was rather shocking at first, just how hard it was for people to really look at what drove them to orgasm. Then I realized they had no tools, no map, no hand-holds to get through the gate-keepers into the deeper territory of their Eros. They knew it was there, they wanted in, but were perpetually stuck at the threshold.

This stuckness is a cultural malaise that stems from a sex-negative moral imperative so severe, we do not even realize we are living in a sexually disembodied and disconnected state. We are an overly "heady" culture that lives from the neck up. We are simply not taught to access the wisdom of the body, our emotions, our sexual depths and the potent imaginal, creative, symbolic dimensions of consciousness.

Here are some simple practices I offer many of my clients, to start to flesh out their own Personal Erotic Myths, and access the deeper dimensions of their sexual imagination.

The premise is that you have an erotic persona(s) as distinct and unique as a fingerprint. It is an authentic, true presence whenever your sexual desire is aroused. It has a definite agenda and personify-cation when aroused, things it says, tone of voice, attire, setting, other counterpart personas to your own, unique body language et al. It is embedded in a story, or more precisely, a Personal Erotic Myth.

If you have no clue, can see no picture, hear no voicings, do not know the story – just start with what you do know.

Say a heterosexual male client knows he will grab a female partner's hair while fucking her from behind and has found himself saying things like, "Take it bitch!" in those last moments before he orgasms. Prior to that finale, he and his sexual partner had gyrated passionately but silently, except for the sounds of breath and plea-sure. Afterwards they do not review this brief, frenzied, wild culmi-nation of sexual exchange, nor acknowledge that it was there at all. My client though, gets the sense it turns his partners on as well.

With this much established, a meditative inquiry can begin. The technique used is a variation of the "Voice Dialogue" process psy-chologists use to help access sub-personalities in their clients. We all have sub-personalities and they are always chattering away below the surface of our daily life. Many of these can be quite negative in the judgments and harsh pronouncements about who we are, our sexual desires, our worth, intelligence, desirability, morality and such. For some reason we find it harder to hear the positive persona messages that are also part of who we are, and in particular the personas alive in us that carry our sexual truth.

Consider that the part of my client that shows up (embodies), pulling his partner's hair when he nears orgasm is his erotic sub-personality. Consider that this part knows precisely the answers to any questions he has for it, and this part is not at all bashful about expressing the truth. And if asked, this part of his psyche may reveal itself in full, explicit detail. For instance, "who" is this bitch, why is she a bitch, what is she saying back, where are you, how did you meet? This is an inquiry that can begin to drill down into the erotic story that showed up and literally drives one to the frenzied finale of orgasm.

The idea of this exercise is not to creatively make up your inner erotic myth. It is to observe and listen to what your erotic persona may tell you about itself, and the what, who, where and how of its desires.

You can try this yourself. Here are some questions to get the inquiry going. Or make up your own.

- *How old is your ideal Erotic Counterpart (EC) ? …and you?*
- *What are they wearing?*
- *What kind of location are you in?*
- *What compelled your EC to be there with you?*
- *How long have you known your EC?*
- *Is your EC provocative or innocent?*
- *Who has more power?*
- *Are there any props or implements of any kind?*
- *What are you saying to your EC?*
- *What is your EC saying to you?*

This type of inquiry can also draw out unconscious parts of you that object to your desire. It can be instructive to listen to or feel into and note these parts as well. These are the resistant parts that to greater or lesser extent are tangled up with your desire, that only allow your desire to stretch so far, if at all. These carry undercurrents of shame, fear, and doubt into your erotic expression, and can inhibit if not shatter your erotic experience, physically, emotionally and spiritually.

Just becoming aware of these anti-sexual inner judgments and anxieties can go a long way to reducing their impact. And it can open the way for more intensive personal work you may take on to begin untangling these inhibiting parts from your authentic sexual expression.

I imagine many might find this type of exercise absurd or weird. If I started talking to other parts of myself, if there were such a thing, and they started talking back to me, that would seem to indicate I am certifiably loony, right!

My experience is that it is more loony to ignore the need and opportunity to differentiate the rich many-faceted complexity of who I am, rather than leave that complexity in what may be a tangled-together, confused, unfulfilled mess.

If you are skeptical that it is possible to separate your aware self from another distinct part of you, and listen to what it might have to say, you might just approach it as an experiment. Verify that it doesn't work, or does.

This is an imaginal process, not a rational one. The imaginal view is accessed through a sense of openness, mindfulness, symbols, archetypes, imagination and other departures from rational analysis. These "irrational" techniques are the keys to drawing into our awareness meaningful content offered up from an inquiry into the symbolic world of our unconscious. We don't return from such an inquiry with a mathematical formula, but with a symbolic one. By letting go of critical intellectual judgment and just "listening", the "voice" of our Eros may have offered up meaningful insight that had not been glimpsed before. We may find that our awareness can now sense a deeper connection and understanding of our authentic Eros.

I will say, the key to this type of imaginal process is to enter a deep state of listening. If you have other thoughts, judgments, anxieties and such about the future or the past, while you are "listening", you are not in a very deep state of listening! To listen, means being in a state of consciousness called, "presence". You are totally here in the moment. You feel deeply connected to your body, not in your head, racing through a barrage of past and future oriented inner banter, if not outright anxieties about things that have nothing to do with right now. It is not necessarily easy to do this. So be patient. It is really an ongoing practice to develop.

To stay focused on listening, it is helpful to have a conscious stated intention to just listen, and to whom you are interested in listening to. During your inquiry, anytime you notice your awareness is starting to drift along a thought stream not connected to your intention, take a deep breath, reconnect with your intention and begin again. Go back to your inquiry.

Listening intently, if you are like me, can be challenging, be it for an inner personal journey or in a discussion with anyone in your day-to-day life. I wasn't even aware of the process of listening, until I was in my mid 40's. That was when I had the shocking revelation – I never listen to anybody! It never occurred to me that I was not a listener. I was always in the mode of thinking about what I would say in response to someone else's thought. I most often, would not let people finish their thoughts, before I would take off on my own again. This was a very embarrassing revelation for me. And I was missing out on the amazing benefits that I later discovered of applying listening to my inner world as well as my outer.

Another key is to allow your sexual persona you are intending to inquire about to operate like an individual and separate entity. This part of you may have been hidden or obscured, shamed judged or feared for decades. It may not be so eager to come into such clear view. This is where an imaginal technique called Voice Dialogue comes in. It is the process of differentiating one part of your psyche from another. This technique is designed to make it possible to talk, and more importantly, listen to this part of you. You can let your aware-self let your sexual persona know how fascinated you are to finally talk. You can express gratitude and admiration. Make it feel welcome. Then you can ask it questions. Ask what it might want to talk about. Whatever comes to mind.

Very important as well is to consider the ambience of the space you will do your inner inquiry in. This is pretty straightforward.

Make it as quiet, comfortable, soothing and inviting as it can be. Then get yourself comfortable, close your eyes, begin slow easy breaths, and imagine you are traveling in your imagination to the perfect spot to meet up with your Erotic persona. Some people, myself included find it helpful to listen to an entrancing rhythmic drum beat. When you arrive at the perfect spot, ask if they or anyone else are open to talking, and let the inquiry begin.

Some people find it helpful to journal if they have learned meaningful information they want to retain.

These and any other techniques that come to you can help you start to glimpse the inner storylines or myth(s) that your erotic persona rides to orgasm, or other deep erotic state. You might find it helpful to take my anonymous online *Discover Your Personal Erotic Myth Survey* for a more in-depth inquiry: GalenFous.com/pem. You can also review the graphic results of a few thousand others who have also taken the survey. Your participation also supports my research into the nature of Fetishsexuality, and I would greatly appreciate and welcome your participation.

Archetypes, Symbols and the Mythic Psychological Structures of D/s- BDSM
Understanding the compelling psychological undercurrents of our most taboo Fetish desires and relationship structures

I believe a Fetishsexual's deepest fantasies are shaped from the interplay of erotic plot lines, archetypal personas and symbolic elements embedded within their sexual psyches. If not yet conscious, these sexual personas and their attendant mythic stories are lurking in the background during our sexual engagements. Bringing these subtle but potent elements into conscious awareness can open us to explosive Erotic intensity, deep seated emotions, and ultimately strengthen intimacy and trust between partners.

The challenge can be to acknowledge these deeper, more vivid dimensions of our fantasies. They are often obscured by the shame, fear or trauma we may have grown up with. No one has ever taught nor encouraged us to look at our sexual expressions with curiosity, hunger or excitement. Too often the most wild, intense, authentic and perverse dimensions of our Eros never see the light of day.

To help in this regard, there are certain tools and techniques you can use, that support you in discovering and inviting in what is personally authentic and meaningful to your sexual expression.

Before I go into to the details about the mythic, archetypal, symbolic structures of D/s-BDSM, I want to speak further about various techniques to access and fully experience them in a healthier, conscious manner.

Learning these techniques, sometimes called ritual practices, can begin to open the internal Erotic pathways you seek to experience. They can help you gain awareness of the physical, emotional, and ecstatic sexual undercurrents within your own experience and with your partners.

These tools, techniques and practices can bring you into a deeper connection to your intention, embodiment, intimacy, and communication between yourself and a partner. Each of these aspects is critical for the journey into a conscious D/s-BDSM exchange.

Creating a clear intention, for your relationship, your life or a single scene is a very important practice. I view a stated intention as rock solid truth. I know it is true, because I created it from an aware place. If I get blown off course to one degree or another, it is my anchor I come back to and begin again.

"My intention is to be as conscious a man as I can be." Is that true? Yes! Undeniably! An intention describes an ideal state. I know I cannot achieve my intention to perfection. I can only move down the path towards it. There is no perfection to attain, but I can make strides in the direction I am aiming. Having a clear intention allows me to create personally meaningful practices or rituals that support my intention and diminish what resists my intention.

A couple in a D/s relationship could create the mutual intention, for example, to aspire to the highest ideals of their respective positions as Dominant and submissive and bring these qualities to the relationship.

They could design practices and protocols that are meaningful to both that support their intention. For example they might establish a protocol to have a respectful, supportive, forthright review of their progress once a month. This creates an opportunity to share experiences, struggles and renew their individual and shared commitments to each other and their intention. Rituals such as this can be a process that connects each partner to the aspects of character or soul they each aspire to. It can be a most intimate and loving way to share vulnerabilities and deepen bonds.

Rituals are simply tools to focus our attention. They help bring our aspirations to a deeper, consistent awareness. They offer the potential to help us discover and heal reluctant, protective, traumatized unconscious parts of us that may be holding us back or resisting our aspirations.

Developing a practice that encourages honest vulnerable communication between partners can go a long way towards helping each partner resolve these inner conflicts and bring a sense of empowerment for both.

Some places along this journey to authenticity may inevitably be of a complexity best worked through individually, with a skilled facilitator or therapist that understands how to work in these realms of personal inner conflicts.

If my intention as a Dominant is to be in integrity (walking my talk), accountable for my actions, or be a wise leader, I have to be aware of, acknowledge and examine all aspects of the ways I may not be in integrity, accountable or in leadership. I need to learn to examine and address the underlying reasons why I may be falling short in these regards.

To better stay on my path, I find it helpful to have personal practices that support me to be more focused and committed to my intention. I have a regular regimen of personal practices to help keep me embodied, present and engaged with my intention. These consist of various movement, mindfulness and imaginal techniques. I try to use communication and listening skills that allow vulnerable honesty for both my partner and myself. This encourages us both to own mistakes and make corrections, to apologize, to ask for support or forgiveness when due.

For me these are lifelong practices. I look at it as being on a journey not seeking the destination. My intentions are ideals that I will never achieve to perfection, but I can keep moving towards them, and renew my efforts when I stumble. And while I still stumble often, it is a much smoother path to get back on track with my intention.

These types of practices are generally simple to understand, and easy to put into practice. They are meant to be personalized, shaped in a way that makes them meaningful and effective for you. There is no magic in them other than the results produced by consistent practice. The challenge is to remain consistent in one's personal practices, similar to how one might approach a personal workout regimen.

Another important potential of using ritual techniques or practices is accessing what I call the realm of the sacred or your own soul.

In my view, something is sacred when it has tangible meaning for me personally. I can feel it, it moves me, it activates strong emotion or bond. What is sacred in my view is entirely personal. It does not come from following dogma or a tradition.

For something to be sacred, it needs to be meaningful to the individual in the present time. It must resonate from a deep place within oneself. Our relationships to our partner's, children, families, communities, professions, creative passions, aspirations, advocacies, activist efforts and more can be recognized as sacred vows or bonds for many of us.

Because the sacred is personal, it may be quite different for different people. The sacred can only be experienced through feeling tangibly connected physically, emotionally, soulfully, and/or spiritually to another person, experience, practice, aspiration, symbol or artifact that is personally meaningful. In other words what is sacred is only defined within your own context. But it often merges as well, with a similar sense and reverence for the sacred within others in the gene pool. This is how tribes are formed.

I believe it sacred to allow everything that is true about myself both dark and light, to have a safe, welcoming place to exist, to be witnessed, encouraged, explored, expressed, honored, healed and loved, in a way that respects the rights and humanity of others. I believe the word I give to others and the agreements I make are sacred. I believe following the codes I honor as a man, is sacred.

When you understand what is sacred to you, then you can develop practices that support your mission and intention within your relationships, and in life.

In the realm of sexuality, I consider it sacred to engage and encourage my desires and those of my partner fully, free of shame, fear or judgment by others. It is the grandest celebration of our souls to express our sexuality honestly and passionately.

Another important concept to consider is that of a "container."

In a ritual sense, a container is simply a specific space you create to hold a part of your experience you want to focus on. A container can be created within your consciousness or it can be an actual physical space. In the general hubbub and tumult in the "container" of our everyday life, it can be more challenging or even impossible to deeply focus on the things we desire and aspire to.

Creating a distinct ritual container, separated from the hub-bub, offers an environment that through its design, intention and ambiance, allows you to explore things in a more focused, fully present way.

The concept of a container can be used for instance for the space where you hold your sexual expression of D/s-BDSM.

This "container" is the real physical space you create to hold your sexual explorations in, as distinct from other spaces in your environment. Depending on how much space you have, you can physically develop your ritual space or container in the moment, or more permanently, in your home. It does not need to be perfect in any way. You want it to feel as "safe" and private as possible. You make the container able to be "sealed" as tightly as possible, so unnecessary or unwanted things or energies don't "leak" out or in.

You fill it with personally resonant ambience - lighting, aroma, sound, music, and texture that will enliven your senses. These resulting sensations help activate more of your body, bringing your natural presence to your awareness. You can adorn your space with personally sacred objects - things that symbolize your passions, what or who is important to you, or what you aspire to, or a memento of a meaningful experience or transition.

These sacred objects/symbols in your ritual space will resonate with corresponding aspects that reside within your unconscious or with your conscious intentions that chose them. This resonance can also bring you to a deeper state of aware aliveness. The right ambiance can help shift you from a scattered, distracted or anxious state to one that feels more soothed, calm and aware.

You can fill your ritual space with the ambiance that encourages your conscious intention to heal, grow, express, explore, connect or whatever your intention may be.

All of these ritual tools can help you be more creative, connected, embodied, and insightful during your sexual excursions into D/s-BDSM play, or in a heartfelt honest discussion about an important issue with your partner.

There is an important distinction to be made here, between the paradoxical way the Dom/sub relationship aspects and BDSM Erotic aspects of this lifestyle operate. Understanding this sublime paradox of the sacred/profane dimensions they represent can allow an exquisite dance between partners.

The D/s side of the paradox holds all the day-to-day interactions, negotiations, protocols, agreements and practical real world considerations for the relationship.

This D/s aspect can also represent the protocols and commitments that would allow a mythic, noble, sacred connection between Dominant and submissive to convene.

In this mythic sense the Dom can be aspiring to their personal ideals of the good King/Queen or similar archetype. For thousands of years of human history in the traditional mythic stories of all cultures throughout the world, the archetypal figure of the King/Queen is universal, as is the servant or devotee.

The mythic heroic stories of a culture and the archetypal personas of King, servant and numerous others populating the story, are like a template drawn from the collective mind. It gave a sacred blueprint for an individual or a culture to follow, to be in accord with that time and place. It appears that each human carries versions of these universal archetypal templates within their own conscious/unconscious structures that are personalized when expressed.

The noble good King/Queen archetype generally symbolizes a leader who blesses, protects, inspires, is wise, makes clear agreements, holds boundaries cleanly, is in integrity, accountable, just, responsible and many other qualities.

The submissive, the loyal devotee, one-in-service archetype, represents the powerful ideals of surrender, devotion, obedience, service, selflessness, and more.

In support of these aspirations in the D/s aspect of the relationship, and to symbolize the shared bond between Dom and sub, bestowing a new name/identity on your submissive can be a potent ritual to perform. Renaming can represent an alchemical act of transformation, turning the lead of previous identity into the refined symbolic gold you desire and now possess. It is a meaningful expression of your authority, your domain, your province to choose the identity for your submissive, that is most meaningful to you, but more importantly to both. The name should come from the inspiration your submissive's very soul evokes within you. A new identity can also symbolize removal of the mask that one hides behind to protect vulnerable secreted parts of their sexuality or other aspects of their being. Energetically, this aligns in a similar way with ancient spiritual traditions where a guru gave a new name to a devotee to symbolize the shedding of their old identity.

Many Dominants and subs in the scene also take on a symbolic name before they are partnered. While this is often for protection of privacy, it also represents some aspect of character or an existing mythic figure they aspire to emulate.

I bestowed the name Angeluna on my partner, based on aspects of her being that I experienced. The Angel aspect denotes her qualities as my fierce devoted guardian, the miracle of her sweet presence in my life, and the ephemeral mystery of her spirit. The luna aspect holds many powerful meanings. The moon is the feminine principle that effects the tides, and creates the ebb and flow of life. The moon has a dark mysterious side, and a light reflective side. The moon waxes and wanes eternally as do the cycles of life and relationship. Angeluna combined brings the sense of spice, the heat and sexual passions of the hot-blooded tribes. A woman on fire, wild and explosive in contrast to her cool headed moon woman.

There of course can be the shadowy counterparts to any name given or other names and qualifiers utilized in the inner chamber of

Erotic-BDSM that may annihilate and reduce one's identity to the basest level.

As in a collaring ceremony, a naming ceremony can be a meaningful ritual that bonds Dominant and submissive together in a deep and meaningful way. Like any ceremony, make it creative and personally relevant to your own way of being, not a formula you read about.

Having the intention to be in my nobility as Dominant to my submissive, brings all the ways I may not be being so noble into closer view as well. The parts of me that withhold, hide, mask, project or act-out unresolved feelings or desires, are what I consider my shadows. These shadow parts of me, and their associated behaviors are not consistent with my values and my intended conduct in the day-to-day relationship.

If I show up in my "Tyrant" (shadow of the King), in the day-to-day aspect of the relationship, then I am being out of integrity with my stated code of conduct. If I am projecting something onto my partner that is not about her, that is bringing out my irritation, impatience, aloofness or harshness, then I am no longer being present or in integrity. Our shadow behaviors are generally designed to protect or deflect attention from some wounded or vulnerable part of our psyche that we have not yet dealt with in a conscious way.

When I am triggered into one of my shadows, I am no longer objectively listening. I am misinterpreting data, and weaving it to fit my negative "story" inside. I am projecting unconsciously some past experience that wounded me, onto my submissive, in the present situation.

I want to constantly work on myself to heal and resolve my own stuff that I may be bringing into the relationship and not project my issues onto my submissive. I want to have my walk and my talk in alignment with my intention to be a noble Dominant.

With mutual and aligned intentions, my submissive and I can both support being in integrity with each other and with ourselves, and experience this sense of the sacred vows we have made as

Dominant and submissive.

Not everyone may be interested in this level of the journey. But if you go very far down this path you will be facing these same conflicts and paradoxes, and old psychological wounds carried since childhood and the shadows around them. It is helpful to be prepared to do some form of personal work to deal with your own interior conflicts that might be blocking your path somewhere along the journey.

The profane side of the D/s-BDSM paradox, the Erotic BDSM side, holds all that is dark, taboo, forbidden, painful cruel et.al in way that carries a potent Erotic charge for both partners.

To allow for risk aware, pushing-the-edge explorations of these profane energies, the Erotic BDSM aspect can be thought of as being protectively held within the all-encompassing noble codes each partner adheres to in the D/s side of the relationship. These sacred codes of the D/s aspect protect and sustain the soulful, loving, intimacy between a D/s couples, and allows them to safely shine the light into the dark, forbidden underworld of their edgiest fantasies.

This deep central connection allows the partners to enter the enticing realms of the taboo, the forbidden, into layers of pain, suffering, cruelty, degradation, sadism and other, in a way that does not traumatize the core body, heart and soul of each, but in fact increases trust, intimacy and fierce erotic ecstasy.

These two metaphorical and paradoxical aspects of D/s-BDSM are the interior landscapes where you hold, protect and nurture yourself, your submissive and the relationship, in ways both Light and Dark.

It is my experience that these two aspects of D/s and BDSM are joined in a way that is paradoxically sacred and profane both.

Sacred and profane are the yin/yang of D/s and BDSM. Both aspects need to be untangled from each other, and allowed separate contexts so that both aspects can fit tightly together, express fully and not be diminished or inhibited by the other. This can allow them to flow seamlessly back and forth as is right for the moment, with clear negotiation, without confusion or emotional harm.

This why there are the two "containers" required, as I approach it, to hold the moral, ethical, soulful and spiritual paradox of the sacred (D/s aspects) and profane (Dark Eros/BDSM aspects) of this lifestyle. The two separate, but concentric containers, allow both the sacred and profane energies to co-exist together, in their full polarity, in a way that is honoring, safer, more clear, transparent, enriching, and authentic for both.

To use a male Dom female sub lens, there can be rich and meaningful protocols, ceremonies and rituals created that connect to you and your submissive's deepest yearnings. Others can be designed to help resolve your deepest fears, and begin healing old psychological wounds. You have the power to create personally meaningful rituals that tangibly feel sacred and soulful. Rituals can be fashioned that are healing, honoring and empowering to both the Dom and sub. Rituals can also be powerful ways to explore and examine parts of us that have been disowned, unresolved, feared, wounded, or significant insights might be revealed from our unconscious through ritual, that were previously flying under the radar.

Embracing a D/s container as a practice for a relationship to develop in, is immersing the relationship in a romantic, erotic mythos that exists beyond the relationship. The myth of the noble, regal, powerful, benevolent Lord (King/Master archetype) and the devoted Lover (Devotee/Loyal Servant/Slave archetype) is an elegant "yarn" to weave a relationship with.

There is no adequate expression for me as a Dominant that captures the feeling of being treated with total adoration, humility and respect by my submissive. Both in the way it feels physically, emotionally and psychically to be held so highly, as well as in my ability to break past my own internal resistance (my shadows and wounds) to receive it.

There is a deep, personal, soulful, physical, emotional, alive connection to this feeling for me. As well as a connection I feel to the collective mythos where these archetypal personas of King/Queen and devotee/one-in-service, and all variations, exist metaphysically.

These mythic stories and personas have been known and used by humans in ritual, and as a mainstay of cultural literature and cosmology, for thousands of years. The universal, collective nature of archetypes and myths has been an integral aspect of all human experience since recorded history, as has been well noted by Carl Jung, Margaret Mead, Joseph Campbell and many others. These multitudes of major archetypes and mythic symbols and stories are shared in common by diverse cultures all over the world. They are part of the human software already embedded in our unconscious.

We may not pay attention consciously to this symbolic dimension of our experience, but we do respond and resonate to these myths, archetypes and symbols in ancient or contemporary form, as we do to symbols of all sorts coming from our inner and outer worlds. Think of how the pixels on the 2 dimensional surface of a screen in a movie theater can be arranged into symbols and stories that evoke authentic laughter, tears, anger and other passions.

Each small ritual act you perform, to high-protocol, ritual ceremonies you create with your partner, can, by design, be rich in meaning to both. These meaningful, emotionally charged rituals help your relationship connections approach the mythic level of the physical, romantic, emotional, mental, spiritual, embodiment of Dominant and submissive.

Imagine a protocol you create that requires your submissive to kneel upon entering your space. They are instructed (and have agreed) to be naked, adorned only in a leather collar. There is no eye contact allowed. They are to crawl and kneel before you, when given permission, head bowed at your feet, ass up, in silence, until given permission to speak.

Consider all that may be going on consciously and unconsciously from this simple yet highly symbolic scenario between Dominant and submissive.

The imposed but voluntary adherence to protocol by the submissive, entering the Dominant's realm, exactly as instructed, is rich in mythos. In this brief scene as Dominant and submissive, we are both immersed in a number of archetypal pairings and counterparts, dancing together on a number of levels within the psyche.

Embodying and expressing these mythic D/s pairings can strike deep chords that seem to be right from the core of my soul. It is through physical embodiments and gestures that things we feel deeply are expressed. The body is naturally imbued to send and receive these Dominant/submissive signals and physical gestures, as part of our instinctive natures.

When I experience this level of surrender from my submissive, I feel beheld in a mythos beyond our personal mythos of D/s. It is a familiar feeling, like I know about this, but not from conscious experience. It feels sacred. It is physically, emotionally, spiritually, authentic, real, and tangible. It is rich in symbolic nuance. These meaningful and intentional ritual symbols a D/s couple invoke can activate strong emotional connections within both partners.

First there is the symbolism of the submissive crossing the threshold of her Dominant's realm (container). The threshold is an important place. It divides the container into what is outside and what is inside. It is a place of choice. It is a place for the submissive to pause, take a breath and connect deeply with her intention in crossing the threshold. The threshold is a place to invite in what will support the submissive's intention, and exclude what does not. It is a place to be in gratitude for what awaits across the threshold. Here the submissive can do a small ritual meditation protocol - to pause, breathe, get grounded in intention, let go of unnecessary, distracting thought, before entering and kneeling.

Witnessing my sub's impeccable obedience and devotion as she respectfully enters my realm resonates a deep sense of trust within me. Her surrender symbolizes and consequently generates the emotions accordant with being honored through the keeping of agreements, even challenging ones, with grace and style.

There is no resistance. Only devotion, and the desire to please are evident in my sub's body language, crawling to kneel and bow before me. Part of me feels physically and emotionally disarmed, tender, even awed. I feel the tremendous trust my sub displays so vulnerably, and a sense of the sacred responsibility that trust implies.

There is the relief, ease, and satisfaction of knowing my sub is surrendered and will not require correction or discipline, won't act out in a way that disrupts the intoxicating flow and romantic beauty of complete power exchange.

The way her body moves towards me in its crawl evokes an animal nature. This grace of movement and the physical vulnerability of the final ass-up pose, stirs my own animal nature. Some primitive, predatory Eros is in play in my body and soul.

Seeing the shape and pose of my sub's body at my feet, is a powerful visual symbol of her surrender. It is a classical, but profane embodiment of prone devotional gestures, organic to human nature and protocol in temples, churches, monasteries and castles of the realm for many ages past. The ass, arched in sexual submission, offering an invitation, is another potent image. To be treated so reverently, to have my sub totally, vulnerably available for use, nurtures and enlivens my sense of power and control.

My submissive is fully exposed and vulnerable at all levels, at my whim, pleasure and mercy. I feel appeased.

This humble pose by my sub on the floor before me represents one in devotion, service and Eros. This resonates with the counterparts of these aspects within me. I take in the truth that I am worthy of this devotion, that I AM the one above, being elevated, the one being served.

The deepest feeling for me in the acceptance of her offering is one of humility and grace, not inflation. My body, emotions and soul feel imbued with the birthright of my Dominance.

Many Dominants (myself included) and submissives carry unresolved parts within the psyche that may be blocking them from more fully experiencing their chosen place in the relationship. Ritual practices I use, help me to get closer to allowing more of these powerful emotional and physical feelings to flow into my body and awareness without restraint. This is the experience of being present, authentic and alive in the truth and intention of the moment.

Making it a conscious practice to pause, breathe, open and receive this offering from your submissive can lead to a deeply satisfying sense of empowerment.

Sometimes it is helpful to notice unconscious, subtle resistances (feelings of shame, unworthiness, past traumas) that limit fully embracing one's Dominant and submissive or attendant sexual natures. Depending on the complexity of what resists your intention, professional sex-positive, kink-friendly guidance may be the best choice to resolve some of these conflicts.

My submissive, when bowed in surrender at my feet, also embodies and symbolizes the physical energetic of the beta or of prey. In the animal world there is a natural point of surrender between predator and prey. A transition where fighting for survival/ control by the prey, transforms to a physical embodiment of surrender and vulnerability.

The Dominant and submissive are reenacting nature's ritual of predator/prey and/or alpha/beta mammalian pack rituals. Resistance and the fight have ceased. The "prey" or beta instinctively exposes vulnerable parts of the body. The eyes are cast down. Any physical movements are meek, stripped of all expressions of aggression or challenge. The Dominants' body language will express this same attitude from their side of the instinctual equation.

How deeply either experience this instinctual psychological state depends on how deeply each has resolved the unconscious restraints in the physical and emotional body. These restraints hold back the natural authentic expression of what is being felt. They are actually the counter embodiments and physical resistance of deep psychological shame and fear, masking and literally holding back the instinctual response.

The instinctual postures expressed in D/s-BDSM are part of our biological, psychological heritage from reptilian forward. The body language gestures conjured from these ancient aspects of the psyche are pre-wired in the autonomic nervous system. Each partner's body instinctually responds just like any other predator and prey would in nature. It is not thought about. It is instinctual.

In my experience I can feel these aspects of my evolutionary heritage alive in me. My animal instinctual nature is still an inherent part of me. The symbol of my submissive posed before me rouses this instinct, it feels powerful and sacred to be aware of and embody these aspects of my psyche.

These wild, untamed, primitive, instinctual aspects of who we are still resides within us. No matter how civilized we might consider ourselves to be, these instinctual responses in our bodies and unconscious, are very much intact and operate in us daily.

The submissive can also represent an object. As Dominant, I have the negotiated power to make my submissive a sacred or profane object.

As a sacred object, I am moved to treat my sub with a certain reverent tenderness. My desire is to bless and protect, while also expecting to be royally served. This is not just some abstract concept in my head. I am connecting emotionally and physically with these inherent archetypal erotic personas.

As a profane object my submissive becomes the symbolic counterpart of my darkest urges. In the realm of Dark Eros these urges are linked to taboo mythic stories alive in my unconscious that can be called up. The lead characters are paired in a sharply polarized relationship. They can range across a pantheon of potential Fetish pairings such as daddy or mommy/ daughter or son, teacher/student, rapist victim, Tyrant Master or Mistress/worthless slave or many other dyads.

One tangible embodiment that I have experienced is the archetypal persona of "Daddy". It is strongest in me, when the counterpart is also alive in my submissive. In one example of this mythos there is an aspect that transcends the taboo Erotic content. The Daddy's little girl totally loves and adores him. She knows she needs to be obedient and is eager for Daddy's love and affection. She gives affection freely and generously. My "Daddy" persona feels drawn right from my soul in a ritual moment like this. I may not shift the core of my energy or embodiment as her Dominant, which would be quite possible to do, but a significant portion of my embodied content may be channeling this Daddy archetype.

Connecting with this "Daddy" part of my psyche is emotionally powerful and enriching. On the one hand, the feeling of tenderness and love evoked is authentic and intense. Who could Daddy love more than his little girl, especially when she is being so devoted, adoring, vulnerable and pleasing?

The point is, the feelings and experience of the archetypal Daddy/daughter dynamic is authentic in the moment. Even though this embodiment is not intended to be considered true in the reality of everyday life, in the ritual container, both Dominant and submissive can have exquisitely potent experiences of the Daddy/daughter mythos together.

Accessing this Daddy archetype has served at times, as an unanticipated gateway for me to reconnect with my true tenderness and affection. Deep feelings of tenderness and care that I may have been holding back or disconnected from in some way in day-to-day life can flow more readily.

To be clear, I am talking about imaginal ritual archetypal experience only. In absolutely no way am I condoning, real life sexual interactions between parents and children, or any adult and children.

Connecting with these internal archetypal parts of our Erotic psyches in ritual with our partners is a sacred act, as I view it. If done with transparency and intention there is the potential to transform and resolve ways we may be holding back our deepest feelings for each other. It can help open up emotional blockages and allow deeper levels of emotional intimacy and free expression.

But the tender aspects I can experience as "Daddy" can also shift into the dark taboo edge of Daddy/daughter interaction. This is the Erotic BDSM space where I can embody my tyrant, sadist, predator and other dark archetypal forces, that thrills into turning my "daughter" into a whore, a rape-toy, a pain slut and other degrading and inappropriate depictions.

When done in a way that is negotiated clearly, with awareness of emotional, physical and spiritual safety, the verboten excursions into the dark edges of forbidden desire can offer both partners an experience of exquisitely charged Eros.

Beyond the Daddy/daughter dynamic within the Erotic BDSM realm and with negotiated consent, my submissive can be totally objectified, stripped of rights and entitlements, a target of pain, degradation, brutality, and cruelty. Within the safety we have created through our sacred D/s protocols and agreements, I can unleash my own shadowy dark desires as superior, all powerful, ruthless, disdainful, disrespectful, asshole, motherfucking tyrant and any other energies that I carry in me.

It is an astoundingly liberating psychological and emotional experience to allow these dark aspects of my soul to be witnessed and expressed. To shine the light on them, to no longer hold them back, after having regularly regulated and suppressed them in everyday life, offers me an indescribable sense of integration and wholeness.

The fact that my submissive is able to hold space for these shadow parts of me, and even beg for them to be unleashed, leaves me feeling awe at this intimate, taboo level of surrender. So that even in the midst of some cruel rampage upon my sub's body and persona she is entwined with me in the Light. I am at moments so awed by this paradoxical tenderness I feel for my partner. To be so loved and honored and encouraged to show all of me, even these darkest edges, is the ultimate intimacy.

Another level of symbol and imagery in the scenario I described earlier connects to the carnivorous animal heritage still present in our instinctual body and psyche. Letting your wild, savage, beast hunt, take down, bite into the back of the neck, or overpower activates survival level, eat or be eaten instincts, emotions and body language. These are a predator's natural responses to hunger, and the need to dominate its hunting grounds to survive.

To feel these instincts alive in your body and psyche is awakening deep connections and awareness of how complex and layered our experience can be. The wild, primitive, "uncivilized" and predatory responses within our psyche can be consciously exercised/exorcized in the ritual container of Erotic BDSM.

These inner instinctual explorations can also help bring greater awareness of how we let these shadowy energies loose in the outer world, in many unconscious, non-consensual ways. Understanding and coming to terms with these paradoxical complexities stirring in our inner realities can lead to more transparent communication and potent interactions in our relationships, in our edgiest sexual explorations, and in our interactions in the everyday world.

There is also an important note I want to make clear. Except for the mildest forms, humiliation and degradation are what I consider edge-play. Degradation and humiliation edge-play requires a lot of self-evaluation, communication, trust, and deep connection between the Dominant and submissive. There are real emotional traumas many of us carry, around self-worth, intelligence, competence, confidence, body image, and more. These aspects require clear boundaries to be defined to protect their unresolved energies from being released unintentionally

Humiliation and degradation play is not a place to rush into or take lightly. If you do find areas of consent that feel safe and choose to explore these edgier places, these scenes can carry an intense emotional, physical, sexual catharsis.

One of the keys here is to negotiate clearly about use of language and personifications agreed on in your Erotic BDSM explorations with your partner.

This means inquiring about any language boundaries your partner may want. The areas to get clear about will generally include language around body image, worthiness, intelligence, gender, femininity, race, religion or other!

Some submissives can be wildly turned on by the explicit degrading language invoked in any of these areas. Others will inevitably carry real life experiences of abuse, bullying or trauma in one of more of these categories. In these cases, certain languaging can easily re-trigger emotionally wounded and sensitive areas for your submissive. These are places to take care and caution.

The intent is to heighten and maximize the Erotic charge through pitch-perfect explicit dialogue, body language et al., not traumatize and wound your partner emotionally.

You may be surprised at how edgy your partner craves this level of degrading language. It may be very focused on some aspects, but off limits in others. Negotiating this territory with precision can keep you both safe, and open you to the depths of psycho-sexual ecstasy you both crave. Again a good principle to follow is to start slow and ease into this complex but compelling terrain. And of course have extensive and explicit negotiations about what is and what is not in bounds.

Certain submissives can find intense degradation play a gateway to an intoxicating freedom. There is a blissful transcendent feeling for many, derived from surrendering control of all the efforts generally applied to maintain the ego identity. "My Dom made me do it!" can be a liberating refrain. Letting go of the façade that one often hides behind and works so hard to maintain can be a tremendous relief.

Our ego-identity also includes all of the civilized psychological structures in place intended to separate us from our mammalian/ reptilian instinctual identities. We are all so civilized after all!

Descending to a sub-human state opens us to the potent instinctual embodiments of our animal heritage. These fierce physical gestures, primitive vocalizations and emotions of fighting back to exhaustion, defeat, surrender, and acquiescence are leading to an exquisite sense of physical and emotional depletion. This is the paradoxical state of bliss that animal prey are considered to experience, when they surrender to being devoured after the fight/flight option has been exhausted. This bliss can be indescribably visceral and blended with Eros, intoxicating.

Another theme to consider is the barley noted characteristics of the "Sex Creature," Many if not all humans carry this persona as a distinct part of their psychological character. I experience it and have witnessed it in many others as a completely separate persona that lurks in the background of our everyday persona. It has its own POV. It embodies in an entirely different way from our everyday personas. It has its own body language, the way it looks at someone it is revealing itself to, tone of voice, way it speaks, dresses and all manner of personification. It has been astonishing to witness this transformation in many of my own experiences when the Sex Creature morphs the everyday body. It brings meaning to the shamanic concept of shape-shifting. The life force, the glow, the sheer Erotic invitation evoked by the body brings about a stunning attraction and beauty far beyond the range of the everyday persona.

There are so many treasures to be experienced when we open to the psychological depths of our Erotic experience, far beyond the boundaries of conventional friction sex.

If you feel stirred by any of what you learned here, take that as a sign to begin your own intrepid journey into your Erotic Wilderness and resolving all that has held you back.

Anatomy of a Personal Erotic Myth
Part 1 – A Couple's Journey
A WOMAN BRAVES HER FEARS ABOUT HER KINKY DESIRES TO EMBRACE HER FETISHSEXUAL YEARNINGS, BECOME WHOLE AND SAVE HER RELATIONSHIP

Many have asked to understand more about what exactly a Personal Erotic Myth (PEM) is, and how I work with client's desiring to come to terms with their erotic desires in a conscious way. To help get a better understanding of this process, I am offering here glimpses from a case study, over the course of 3 sessions with a recent client. She came with the intention of discovering, understanding and embracing her Personal Erotic Myth, which she had kept secret for decades. This led eventually to my also working with her partner one-on-one.

Her part of the story reveals the challenges and fears she faced to integrate this true and important aspect of her psyche into her everyday life with her partner.

She was a woman in her early 40's, with a particular life-long desire for rough sex, Daddy/daughter play, dressing slutty, and other taboo aspects. She had been unable to reveal or share these desires with past partners. She was currently in an 8-year relation-ship with a man who was very sweet and loving, but was not the aggressive masculine persona who inhabited her sexual fantasies. She had reached a place where she knew her desire was demanding to be expressed, even to the point of leaving her relationship if necessary.

She sought me out for support. With her partner's agreement she was choosing to come to terms with this aspect of her sexuality, on her own, with hopes of then bridging this desire to include her partner, down the path.

She fits with some precision, into my concept of someone whose sexual path to orgasm or other deep erotic state, is driven by a PEM. Her PEM formed decades ago, and, as is the case for many with a Fetishsexual orientation, she was sexually engaged and aware before she had reached puberty.

In my experience working with hundreds of people over the last 15 years, Fetish desires are rarely connected to pathologies generated from early age traumas, or other environmental factors, as many are led to believe. In my experienced based view, a fetish driven sexuality is as innate, inherent and lifelong as is being gay or lesbian.

The work I do with a client in this dimension is often branching into ground-breaking territory, as far as current academic and clinical models of human sexuality and therapy go. What the work looks like will vary according to the individual circumstances of the client.

The main components are an initial discussion to determine what the client wants as an outcome of our work together, some sense of what their sexual desire looks like, what resists or conflicts with their desire, and their relevant personal history. This would include areas of trauma or abuse, as well as the environment and sexual attitudes or moralities they were raised in.

My goal is to encourage them to approach whatever is true sexually from a conscious, risk aware, honest, consensual, negotiated, embodied context. The outcome can be an empowered li-berating engagement and acceptance of their deepest, edgiest desires and a start to resolving the trauma, shame, self-judgment and fear their sexual desire may have been entangled in within the unconscious psyche.

The client and I may work together at a cognitive level to develop an ongoing, practical, clear strategy to move towards and negotiate what the client wants in the real world for themselves, and with a partner(s).

Often, our true sexual natures can be literally tangled up with other parts of us in our unconscious that are locked in intense fears, shames and harsh judgments about our true sexual natures. These were taken on from a sex-negative family, religion and culture as we grew up. They can physically, emotionally and psychically resist our intention to express our desires.

We often carry internalized, harsh moral judgments and stories about our sexuality, our personal worthiness and more. Even as adults, these inner forces can still have power over our desire, and our intention to express our sexuality consciously.

There may be practices co-developed with the client to help them focus on their intention to empower their desire and diminish, heal and resolve the power held by their inner judgments, fears or shames.

There may be other imaginal processes involved to help a client access unconscious material to "flesh" out and bring to precise conscious awareness, the who/what/where of their desires, and similarly with what resists or judges their desire.

Often work will be evident, that wants to be approached at the body level. I support the client in developing practices to help them get present, embodied and grounded. This is usually the starting point for sessions as well. This best prepares the client and myself to be fully engaged and present for whatever other work may follow. And it is very helpful for the client to develop their own personal practices to bring the sense of embodiment and presence in their everyday life.

Exploring at the level of somatic awareness, movement, and other physical practices can also help locate and begin to release the many fears, shames and other tensions that have accumulated in the body. After decades of hiding, judging, or holding the desire back, these physical tensions can be quite pronounced. It is similar with the physical efforts we make to cover up shame or fear or anger. This hiding is a physical act that builds and stores tension. There is a physical gesture that wants to express naturally and there is a counter physical gesture operating to hold the desire back. These tensions and the emotions they have held back can often begin to be relieved through somatic exercises the client can develop or through hands on body level work.

In a deeper layer yet of the work that might open up with a client, and as was the case with the client described here, a negotiated ritual process might be agreed on, where I may in some way and to some extent, embody a mythic counterpart to the persona in the myth that drives the client's desire, that conforms to non-sexual interactions and boundaries standard to my practice.

A PEM can take many forms, but to a great extent will include paired personas in some form of power exchange such as Master/slave, Mommy/son, FemDom/cuckold, Daddy/daughter, Teacher/student, and a pantheon of other variations. Some people identify as "Switches" and can cross back and forth between poles as they wish. One's Personal Erotic Myth generally includes action, dialogue, tone of voice, body language, props, attire and context that can and often fiercely yearns to be expressed. For someone who is a Fetishsexual, it is not acting out a part. It is not just role-playing. It is literally embodying this alter erotic persona that one authentically possesses, and allowing it the unencumbered space to express fully, without shame, guilt or judgment.

These archetypal personas operating within one's PEM are already intact and whole within the individual's personal unconscious but also reference standard mythic personas in the collective unconscious.

In other words many of the erotic themes and archetypal personas that occur in the individual PEM are found globally as well throughout the gene pool. The erotic myths people yearn to express do not need to be cognitively scripted out, they just need to be allowed to embody and be present. These parts of the erotic psyche already know generally what they desire to do, say, wear, with whom, what implements, attire setting and other elements, common to a mythic story.

Work with clients often needs to go this deep, this hands on and interactive, to help them uncover, untangle, heal and embrace their authentic desire and reclaim it from the decades of denial, fear, shame, and hiding, that one's desire may have been pushed down under.

It is incredibly complex as well, for many individuals to maneuver some of the terrains of paradox that are part of the journey. Such as, how can I yearn to be so perverse, taboo, and primitive in my sexual desires and also still be a good parent, partner, or social, political or religious community member? Can I be both sacred and profane without compromising my personal integrity, agreements and physical, emotional, mental and spiritual well-being?

To explore the depths of our darkest desires is a challenging, but empowering and healing process. It requires one to cultivate the deepest intention to become more conscious, aware, embodied, open, honest, curious, vulnerable, fierce, consensual and more.

It is my premise that if these very compelling parts of our sexual natures are kept in hidden, secretive shadowy behaviors, they will inevitably blow up in destructive ways within our family, social and work life.

I feel that we are in an unprecedented era where the soul of Eros is forcing humanity's hand in a way. It's time to fess up, stop pretending we have no wild or dark side….or else the havoc of the sexual shadow (repression, cheating, hiding, porning, sexual violence or other unhealthy diversions) running amuck in the world right now, will get worse.

In the case of my client, cited here, she struggled to resolve the paradoxes within herself and how to communicate and express it honorably and ecstatically with her partner. In her own words, she reveals her experience, discoveries and outcome of our work to come to terms with her sexuality and her relationship with her partner.

Her story offers a comprehensive overview of many of the complexities of expressing one's authentic desire within the self and in relationship, and encountering the shadows, wounds, fears, shames and judgments, that are inevitably part of the process.

In the upcoming part 2 of this article, my client, in her own words, reveals her experience, discoveries and outcome of our work for herself and her relationship with her partner. Her story offers a comprehensive overview of many of the complexities of expressing one's authentic desire, and encountering the shadows/wounds/fears/shames/judgments that are inevitably part of the process.

Here is an excerpt…

"She wants to possess her captor as he possess her. She wants the freedom of having no choice. No will. The power of surrender. She wants to be known and seen in all of her wild and nasty ways. She is Irresistible. Her true power lies in her capacity for seduction, and for surrender. She willingly submits to the man who will possess her, own her. The man to whom she belongs. The man she has given herself to. The man who loves her. Who is himself unable to control his desire for her. Who must possess her every which way he can. Who will show her off. Share her with whomever he pleases. For she will do as she is told. "

ANATOMY OF A PERSONAL EROTIC MYTH
PART 2 – HER VIEW

A CLIENT CHOOSES TO EXPLORE THE DEPTHS OF HER SUBMISSIVE SEXUAL KINK AFTER KEEPING IT HIDDEN FOR DECADES. HER RELUCTANT "NICE GUY" FIANCÉ SLOWLY WARMS TO HIS OWN DOMINANT COUNTERPART.

"It was incredibly empowering… to reveal the secret desires I had hidden away for decades. I finally met this young girl who has been with me, in my fantasies or mythic desire, as you call it, in nearly every orgasm throughout my life…I felt so enlivened, so awakened by the experience."

A client couple was divided by an unbridgeable erotic mismatch at the start of our work together. The woman had intense life-long sexual desires to submit to an aggressive dominant man. Her partner was taught growing up to treat women with respect and tenderness.

During the course of their work with me, her enlivened passion began to wake up the dominant, sexual masculine within her fiancé. Up until this point, he had been the kind, sweet masculine presence he had been raised to be. While this made for a generally easy-going, loving day to day relationship, it also left his partner's fierce authentic erotic desires unfulfilled. The erotic divide threatened the deep union they both sought with each other.

Their story models the opportunities as well as the complex resistances encountered in bringing our most taboo sexual desires into our personal awareness and then into our relationships. The sexual aspects of this particular relationship happens to fit the male dominant model. I have also worked with couples who aspired to a female dominant model in their sexual expression. Both of these sexual styles, and everything in between occur within the full spectrum of what I call Fetishsexuality, aka Kink or D/s-BDSM.

The personal narrative of her experience begins below. Both her and her partner had just attended a recent Conscious D/s-BDSM workshop I had led. Her thoughts from that workshop and her personal work with me are woven into her reflections.

I feel that her reflections map out well, the inner terrain and operation of her Personal Erotic Myth. A PEM contains the fantasy imagery, storylines, mythic personas, props, attire, dialogue and actions that drive a person who has a PEM to orgasm or other deep erotic states. This mythos is often expressed in Fetish, Kink, and D/s-BDSM oriented sex, where symbol, myth and archetypal personifications abound.

Here is C's story of her journey into her life-long Fetish desires. (In a follow-up email, I had asked her about the sense that something was missing from our previous session.)

"Very perceptive- I appreciate that about you and your work. Yes, something was missing. My mind was wandering and I found myself more than once wanting/wishing that it was my partner who was owning me, possessing me. But I think there was something more, and I don't know what it is.

"One possibility is that I wanted to resist more, to be overtaken, against my will, or to have that sense. In the workshop, I found myself telling L (her partner), that I wanted a simulated rape. I wanted him to chase me down, force me to hold still, tie me up.

"The methodical exploration of limits that you and I have pursued in our sessions has served me, but I sense in this last session, also limited me, or that part of me that I am craving to embody. And afterward I thought, maybe I'm done. Maybe it's time to explore this with my partner, and not on my own.

"At the same time though I should acknowledge that L has been really struggling with feeling that he is not the kind of man that could be what I seem to be seeking. He's been feeling threatened by my attracttion to the strong, forceful masculine. He can get triggered into his pain/wounding of not being good enough. His last partner left him because she needed a man who would push back, give more resistance (be more firmly in his masculine). There seems this tension inside him between being raised by his mother to believe fighting is for animals and a good man is a gentle man. He is a generally kind and gentle being

in the world. These darker elements of his selfhood are there, but have yet to be embodied and expressed in a healthy and conscientious way. But they do leak into our relationship by the occasional explosion of his anger.

"All of this has contributed to my own sense of pulling back from this exploration emotionally. Perhaps that was also at play in our last session. I am feeling some uncertainty, some fear around the cost of my foray into dark Eros, I am feeling less driven to find "her." I'm feeling confused and somewhat out of touch with my longing. I'd welcome some support.

"But, regarding my overall experience. I have so valued the sacred container you have provided for my experience, and the skill and finesse in which you have invited these aspects of my being. The first session was so powerful. I finally met this young girl who has been with me, in my fantasies or mythic desire, as you call it, in nearly every orgasm throughout my life.

"I don't remember having such fantasies when I was very young, as you indicated is often the case, but certainly, from puberty on. My budding sexuality was not embraced or celebrated in any way. I was an early explorer, masturbating by age 5, and soon engaging other little girls to play with me well into puberty.

"But it was always a hidden, shameful thing. I got caught a couple of times. Once at home by my parents, once with a girl friend at her place. Her parent's discovered us in our play, and forbad me from going to her house from then on (I think I was about age 9/10).

"An embedded sense of shame kept me from verbalizing/sharing my fantasy with my first husband or any lover. I was sure something was wrong with me, that I would have to envision being raped or punished against my will, in order to have an orgasm.

"It was incredibly empowering to explore these desires I have had for decades during our initial session. To hear "Daddy" speak to me, to be punished for my transgressions, to submit to his firm but gentle authority was ecstatic. Your tone and pitch perfect inflections whispered to my "slutty little girl" were entirely compelling.

"I felt so enlivened, so awakened by the experience. I met this wanton young girl who could not own her own desire and so incurred the wrath/or desire of those in authority (father, teacher, priest, doctor) to control her, punish her, deliver to her exactly what she wanted.

"Later that eve, I performed the inner dialogue, differentiation ritual you taught me, to bring "her" into clearer focus. It was powerful to ask her what she wanted. And to learn her name: (omitted for privacy). She spoke to me, so clearly, in her own voice.

"She wants to possess her captor as he possess her. She wants the freedom of having no choice. No will. The power of surrender. She wants to be known and seen in all of her wild and nasty ways. She is Irresistible. Her true power lies in her capacity for seduction, and for surrender. She willingly submits to the man who will possess her, own her. The man to whom she belongs. The man she has given herself to. The man who loves her. Who is himself unable to control his desire for her. Who must possess her every which way he can. Who will show her off. Share her with whomever he pleases. For she will do as she is told - willingly, and with a sense of relief. He relieves her of any responsibility for her sexual inclinations or expressions. He controls how she will open to her own desire. He rescues her from her own accountability, responsibility, perhaps from her shame (?). He takes her, takes her like he owns her. He takes care of her, of her sexual needs - which she dare not openly confess - but which he knows and understands. He takes care of her as he would his most precious belonging. And she knows she is safe. She is where she belongs.

"I later came to realize that there were two aspects to this young girl, two different personas. There is the young girl dispossessed of her own desire, seeking the punishment (and pleasure) which she could receive not through her own will and desire, but through her transgressions.

"And there is also the wanton young girl, again overpowered but more of a willing sex slave, who shows up in fantasies of being gang raped or held to serve multiple men's pleasures (e.g., the football team, boys who take her into the back field, the school bus).

86

"I thought I would encounter her again, and looked forward to it with great anticipation, in our second session. But she did not show up. Instead, an angry and ornery woman, fierce and certain of her sexual power showed up, invited by the forcefulness of her restraint.

"No longer that child with no will/ desire of her own, this woman knew her power. She knew her possessor, and, initially, fought him, anger coursing through her body, her voice roaring in primal animal fashion. Subdued by his sure and forceful presence, she gave into her bondage, and I found myself delighted by her beauty, her raw sexual desire, and her capacity to allure and entice desire in her captor.

"I discovered new elements of pleasure playing in my dark Eros: red rope corset, standing shackled, legs free, I felt the sexual charge course through my body, my blood, and I felt a timelessness to this energy. It was not just a part of me I was feeling, but something eternal in womankind. A connection to those brave and beautiful women who were enslaved, forced to submit to their captors, and understanding that was her place, and her power.

"This second session was also a big experience, in a different way. Shackled and restrained, glorious in her beauty, she wanted what she deserved: to be fucked, to be fully taken by her captor.

"In our third session, I went in not really knowing what limits were awaiting to be discovered, what submerged sexuality might be revealed, who would show up. I wanted to imbibe my Eros in a deeper way, and to learn more about my desire, and my limits. My Eros was perhaps even more fully engaged and appeased in our third session, but I did not find that inner power in my surrender.

"This exploration into my shadow, my secret fantasies, my submerged sexual identities, began as a solo journey. I wanted to taste the experience of what was in my head when I orgasm, without having to process or consider my current partner's feelings and fears. When I brought him in to my explorations I was surprised and relieved to hear that he would like to know this young girl in my inner erotic myth, that he wants to love all of me. I knew from the many times he's told me, that he could see her often when we make love. I was encouraged to reveal my fantasies with him as I'd never done with any man before.

"And yet it has not been a straight forward journey. His fears of not being that kind of man, his identity as a kind and gentle man, his desire for tender intimacy seemingly at odds with engagement in any power play. These threatened my sense of safety, even our future as a couple, as he told himself I'm just not that kind of guy, and you may need something I can't give. I found myself realizing I was defending the rights of someone I hardly knew in my brief encounters with her. I found myself wondering just how important this was to me, whether I could just let it go. At the end of the third session a lot of my longing had dissipated, perhaps because of the dichotomy between self-exploration and my love and desire for mutual exploration, which was uncertain at best.

"My partner and I initiated counseling with a therapist known by many in the Polyamory community, and it was helpful to have him explain the healing capacity and possibility of enhanced intimacy and connection that is available through power exchange to my partner.

"We then attended the workshop you facilitated, which provided a safe place for my partner to witness how one might step into power play, and to better understand the necessity and form of creating a safe container and agreements around the exchange. I see new excitement in my lover, and I'm relieved and excited myself to begin to more intentionally and consciously explore this realm with my man.

"And that is where I have arrived as I write of this journey, sincerely grateful for the support and the education you have skillfully and gracefully provided."

In the final segment the story will shift to the view of C's initially reluctant partner and the surprising outcome it lead to for him…and his relationship. Here is an excerpt:

"I would like to meet with you to further C's journey and enjoyment of the BDSM scenes/themes that so draw her. I am only mildly interested in being a top to her, and would like to explore this with you. These three issues seem to be what's holding me back:

1) Fear of rejection if I don't get it right, or if I don't develop a stronger dom-sense.

2) Dismay that we don't find time for prime time sex, and wanting my basic sexual needs and our connection to be satisfied before we embark on a risky project.

3) It looks like a dauntingly large project that takes a lot of pre-planning and learning of techniques."

ANATOMY OF A PERSONAL EROTIC MYTH
PART 3 – HIS VIEW
WHAT DO YOU DO WITH YOUR NICE GUY WHEN SHE BEGS FOR YOUR BAD BOY?

How would you respond to your partner's request for dominating, rough kinky sex?

Our inner sexual yearnings and our intimate relations with our partners are way more complicated than the simplistic, prudish, sexual morality we have grown up with. Here is just one of these complexities that I encounter when working with men, women and couples seeking to embrace their most taboo desires, in a conscious healthy way.

Women's sexuality and its overt, liberated expression is on the rise. It is coming out of the shadows and into the mainstream. For many women this means learning about self-love, intimate touch, sacred sexuality, neo-Tantra, sex toys, g-spots and other meaningful sensual expressions. For others it has a kinkier, edgy expression. This interest in Kink, Dominance and submission and Fetish by millions of women worldwide was recently awakened and revealed by the 50 Shades phenomenon.

Paradoxically the cultural conversation about men's sexuality is seeped in notions of rape-culture, creepiness, and misogyny from the left and immorality, sin and the work of the devil on the right.

Over the last 50 years a great number of men have attempted or were raised to be the nice, sweet, considerate guy. What Robert Bly coined as the "soft male" is a predominate representation of the masculine in these current times. These are men who lost their edge. They gave up their voice. They fail to push back and hold their ground in their relations with women, without manifesting the shadowy tyrant or the weakling. There is a significant population of men whose sexual engagement style is toned way down, consequently, if not shamed into conformity by conservative, religious morality, an emasculating environment and our generally sex-negative culture.

So what should a guy do when their partner grows weary of tepid nice guy sex and demands that he be a brutish predator in the bedroom? If you have not already embraced your conscious good man and your conscious bad boy, here is a story of a man who did, in his relationship with his fiancé.

In parts 1 and 2 of this case study I described the journey of a client couple. They were divided by an unbridgeable erotic mismatch. The woman was at a point that she felt she might need to leave the relationship. I met with the woman initially for several sessions, prior to meeting with her partner. She revealed that her life-long sexual yearnings centered on submitting to an aggressive dominant man…or men. During the course of her work with me, she began to come to terms with her own fears, shames and shadowy unconscious behaviors that showed up around her fetish desires. These desires included fantasies of rough sex, dressing slutty and being gang-raped, or being owned and passed around by her Dominant man. These had been recurring themes in her frequent masturbatory excursions since her early teens.

Now in her mid-forty's she was determined to embrace this mostly hidden, secreted, abandoned part of her sexuality, in a healthy, conscious mature way. This included learning about honestly discussing her desires with her partner, negotiating for what she wanted, reviewing safety issues, safe-words, aftercare and other components of conscious engagement of her fetish desires.

Her newly enlivened and liberated passion began to wake up the sleeping dominant assertive sexual masculine within her fiancé. But part of him was very reluctant, and not sure he could allow himself to let go of his deeply ingrained nice guy embodiment. Up until this moment he had been the kind, sweet soft masculine presence he had been raised to be. He did not believe it was right for a man to be aggressive and dominant. This point had been drilled into him as a boy by his very domineering mother. While this generally made him a very sweet and easy-going partner in the day-to-day relationship, it also left his partner's fierce authentic erotic desires unfulfilled. This divide threatened the long-term union they both sought with each other.

I began work with him one-on-one to support him in bringing his latent but authentic sexual dominance to life, and learning to bring it to conscious, consensual expression.

Here is how he stated his want going forward:

> *"I would like to meet with you to further C's journey and enjoyment of the BDSM scenes/themes that so draw her. I am only mildly interested in being a top to her, and would like to explore this with you. These three issues seem to be what's holding me back:*
>
> > *1) Fear of rejection if I don't get it right, or if I don't develop a stronger dom-sense.*
> >
> > *2) Dismay that we don't find time for regular sex, and wanting my basic sexual needs and our connection to be satisfied before we embark on a risky project.*
> >
> > *3) It looks like a dauntingly large project that takes a lot of pre-planning and learning of techniques.*

Over the course of 3 sessions I supported L (how I will refer to him) in beginning to identify and untangle the unconscious restrictions and internal beliefs he held about his masculine power. He began to understand how his nice-guyness had a shadow side, as well as a noble side. His exploration of the shadow side revealed his fear of stating a strong opinion, a fear of displeasing a woman, of raising a woman's anger. This part of him felt powerless, weak, timid and shy. He was unable to state or hold his own boundaries. He was continually yielding and bending. At times, though, the accumulated resentment from his abdications would cause a brief explosion of anger. He began to understand how he could bring both his sweet, tender side, as well as his assertive masculine into balance, instead of abandoning or holding his own voice back. The next step was to bring this sense of power into the erotic dance his partner so longed to explore with him.

Another area of work that was clear and is often the case, was his lack of body awareness, or presence. His shyness and timidity was mirrored in his body language and movements. I helped him through some movement practices to bring a more fluid, graceful flow into his gestures. This helped smooth out the clunky, unsyncopated movements his body had been stuck in for so long. He learned about staying in his breath and intention to support being present.

I put a leather flogger in his hand. I had him kneel and place a big pillow before him. I asked him to hit the pillow with the flogger. His aim, his control, his power-stroke were all off beat, as would be expected after decades of the restraint he had placed on his body and fierceness. We worked on some mechanics and with some practice, his body eased into a more coordinated and potent swing of the flogger.

In regards the fierceness I suggested he recall his anger at some point along the way with C, where he abdicated his power, his own rights. I could see the spark in his eye and then his body as he made the connection between his right to his personal power, his right to his own want, and the authentic expression of it. This exercise supported an important connection at the physical level. It brought fierceness back into his body, and an authentic emotional expression into his soul that had been withheld.

He said he never felt more exhilarated. To be clear, this exercise was about accessing and embodying authentic fierceness not an old story of anger.

I had already worked with his partner and knew she had shared the practices of negotiation, safe-words and after care required to safely journey into these more primitive instinctual levels of desire.

I also helped him understand how these were two different aspects of their relationship - the day to day loving side of tenderness, respect and care, and the erotic side that was calling for fierce, untamed force and dominance of his partner in a consensual negotiated frame work.

After the first session, I heard back from him via email later in the week.

"I want to share what a great experience I had at our session, how powerful I felt being me, more assertive, more alive, less shy about offending by sharing my opinions. Then a few days later, I had a joyous Dom experience controlling and forcefully spanking my partner during lovemaking, much to her pleasure. Such different roles, and so deliciously fulfilling to be embracing them. The unfolding continues! I am especially interested in learning the talk that C craves, the daddy/teacher/authority figure talk that you demonstrated so well."

In our next session, I offered more about ritual as a practical tool for consciously entering these deeper aspects of the sexual psyche. I explained how creating a meaningful ritual container could support his new intention in engaging his partner.

This self-designed container is his personal domain to rule in, as he desires. He creates the ambiance that best suits him. Ambiance includes, lighting, sounds/music, aromas, textures, and artifacts. It can include how he wanted C to dress, enter the room etc. All of these levels of ambiance enliven the physical senses in a personally meaningful way and thus support being more present and embodied.

I worked further with his embodiment of the dominant, authoritative, daddy persona that was emerging. He did not need to script out dialogue for that persona as much as to allow this innate part of him that was becoming more evident, to be allowed to fully embody in his ritual Erotic engagements with his partner. That part of him already knew what to say and what it wanted. All the parts of him that resisted, judged or felt shame about this aspect of his erotic expression – just needed to get out of the way. His dominant persona, when fully present, knew exactly what it wanted to say, what tone of voice, what physical intensity it might be said with.

He next reported back:

"I had a blast with C last week applying what I learned about creating my own ritual container… having her start the ritual dressed

in my preferred sexy attire and with lighting the fire on her knees, being my footstool, taking off my shoes and socks. I started to feel more comfortable in telling her what to do, what "I" wanted her to do. Seeing her respond so devotedly, being a "good girl" for "Daddy" was amazing, exhilarating. Yeah, it was so good!"

About 6 months after I last saw them, I received an invitation to their wedding. It was a beautiful day in July. The ceremony was a lovely statement of devotion and care for each other and their intention for their life together from that day forth. When I went through the receiving line to congratulate them, I received a big smile and warm hug from C. Then I gave L a hug and he leaned over and said. "Galen, I wouldn't have made it here if not for you, I am a changed man!"

"Thank you, but you did the work, you both did. I just nudged you a bit to find your own path." I replied.

There is a path for each of us to be conscious, empowered, respectful compassionate men and women. Taking this path allows us each to fully embrace the full range of our sexuality from sacred to profane. We just need to do the work to open the gates blocking the path.

WHY MATCHING EROTIC MYTHS ARE IMPORTANT TO SUCCESSFUL RELATIONSHIPS

One of the consequences of our culture's overriding sexual restraint is the cumbersome, outdated dating protocols singles are still expected to follow when choosing a life-partner.

One of the most deeply embedded protocols beseeches partners not to have sex before marriage. This and similar sex-negative moral imperatives have seeped from the religious realm into socialized behavior in the culture at large. While seldom followed, these undercurrents still inhibit many adults from openly discussing, understanding and exploring each other's sexuality while in the initial stages of dating.

Some new couples may go through months and more of dating, before they may engage in any sex at all. And in a great many cases, this means that even a preliminary discussion of what is pleasing or hot sexually is prohibited, as is what is not sought or desired.

In many of these conventional dating situations, couples choose to be in relationship together before they really begin to get a glimpse of each other's deeper sexual truths.

They seek to learn every other detail of who their potential partner is. They want to tangibly experience how their partner inter-acts socially with family, friends and colleagues. They will note all habits good and bad. They want to get clear about every detail for how it would be to travel through life together – except the shape of their sexual desire.

These couples marry or commit, without the slightest clue about what the deepest desires of their partners may look like. They may have pushed the envelope a bit sexually, but if they've stayed within the range of the standard dating protocols, the deeper sexual truths hidden and often so well guarded, have not seen the light of day.

Once partnered, these truths may eventually show up in the relationship with sudden, unexpected "strange" sexual affections one partner wants bestowed or to bestow. This can certainly be upsetting and unsettling in the moment to the other partner. Without having had a preliminary discussion of one's desires and boundaries there is no foundation and mutual understanding or agreement to support the desire. There are no agreements in place to make it feel safe. And a deep sense of safety and trust is critical for partners to share the well-guarded perversity that may burn inside them.

For some, a spontaneous revelation about a particular fantasy may be a titillating break-through that lifts the veil, and gives a peek into the darker caverns of their partner's desires. This may inadvertently and fortuitously stir both partners' wild sexual creatures from slumber.

When our neglected "sex creatures" sniff the presence of desire close by, they can become quite alert, hungry and eager to be fulfilled. If both partners can build trust and feel safe to be open to each other's desires, then they may be able to cross the threshold into a level of sexual honesty that cultural overlays have forbidden.

This is also a situation where desire could be submerged even further, never to be seen again, at least in front of our disapproving partner. The shunned partner then feels the need to keep their desire hidden, alive but secret, and will tend to express it eventually in shadowy, unhealthy ways. Having affairs, online porn sessions, strip clubs, or chat rooms will become the secret avenues of one's sexual expression. This brings an accompanying anxiety about being out of integrity, getting busted, and the fear of the devastating consequences that may bring about.

People from my generation (Boomers), and likely many from the generations that have followed, would never have thought or dared to ask about the explicit sexual likes and dislikes of our partners or spouses. At least not before we committed to the relationship. Nor would our sexual desires have been conveyed before "agreeing" to have sex, however flimsy and barely spoken the "agreements" may have been!

Not considering what our future long-term partner's sexuality looks like, can be as disastrous to the relationship as not knowing beforehand if our partner wants children, how many or at what point in time.

How much confusion, anger and misunderstanding has this lack of communication and honesty about sexual desire created within married or long-term partnerships? How much sexual frustration, cheating, loss of libido, or even pathological disorders have arisen simply because a couple's Erotic Mythos did not match? Even worse, it did match, but neither partner would dare express their desire to the other. Or sexual desire kept getting tangled up with anger or resentment in an aspect of the relationship that had nothing to do with sexual desire, and the denial or granting of sex became a weapon instead of a pleasure.

Thankfully, the vanguard communities of the new sexuality are establishing a foothold in the general population, and encourage open discussion, honesty, tolerance and exploration of whatever aspects of sexual desire both partners agree to.

This is the area where the Kink, Fetish and D/s, BDSM communities have led the way. There is a lot of published info about negotiating with a partner for what one wants and doesn't want in a sexual "scene". A scene is a finite encounter, that a Top and bottom, or Dom and sub negotiate, about what is agreeable, and not, for the scene.

In the negotiating protocols, there are clearly defined boundaries established, safe-words to use for the unexpected glitch, and an honest and specific expression of desires. There is some level of after-care agreed to after the scene is finished. These protocols even apply, or especially apply, to those looking to be in a full time relationship as Dominant and submissive, or other fetish-paired partners.

But these same approaches can and should be applied to any kind of Erotic pairing or relationship, short and long term.

Spontaneous sex, with no stated agreements nor understanding of our partner's deepest desires, can certainly grant a pleasurable release. Getting off usually feels great! Besides the pleasure of friction sex, the release of significant body tension through sexual connection can also lower a sense of "disconnection" that one partner may have felt towards the other. A deeper intimacy in that moment of sex is quite possible between lovers, even without both partner's fully orgasming. With the release of these physical tensions, the internal stories, and the unresolved resentments and judgments each partner may carry about themselves or their partner can momentarily recede to the background.

But if this spontaneous, unspoken sexual expression is as far as the partners venture into Eros together, they are missing out on sharing the rich Erotic myths that were driving their passions in the first place. They could feel "something", but had no idea what the lovely myth of their partner may have been. And allowing this myth to be expressed honestly, instead of hidden, is where the depths of intimacy begin.

There are few things more intimate than to feel safe, loved, welcomed, met, honored, witnessed and exultant for sharing our most secret sexual desires. This is especially true if we have been used to hiding and fearing judgment, if not harsh rejection for whatever our desires may be. There is nothing more sacred and exhilarating than to step into sexual ritual with your partner to freely confess to "Daddy" why a bad girl should have her pussy spanked, or to kneel before your Goddess to let her know how humbled you are to be able to serve her or thousands of variations. To begin to open to your personal Eros that is alive within your sexual soul is to begin to touch upon the depth of Eros.

In order to find a partner with a matching Erotic mythos, it is important to first understand, explore and map our own Personal Erotic Myth.

TAKE THE *DISCOVER YOUR PERSONAL EROTIC MYTH SURVEY*

The *Discover Your Personal Erotic Myth Survey (PEM)* is a tool for individuals or couples to map out the nuanced depths of their sexual desires. Once understood, people can then begin to learn how to fit those desires into their everyday life in a conscious, healthy, fulfilling manner.

Over 2000 people, generally from more sex-positive and sex-alternative populations have taken the survey so far. The results are eye opening and reveal the great depths and variations of sexuality that are emerging in the contemporary world.

My experience working with clients demonstrates that knowing your Personal Erotic Myth can open you to unimagined sexual ecstasy, deepen intimacy in your relationships, and help you avoid disastrous erotic mismatches in long term relationships.

A PEM contains the fantasy imagery, story-lines, mythic archetypal personas (such as Dom/sub Master-Mistress/slave, Daddy/daughter), and the particular enactments that drive a person that has a PEM to orgasm, or other deep erotic states. It is often expressed in Fetish, Kink and D/s-BDSM oriented sex. Some people are quite aware of their PEM, and may have caught glimpses of it, or more, well before puberty…even if they have yet to share it with another. Some may have already crossed the threshold of secrecy their desire may have been held in, to engage the desire itself. Some will have multiple PEM's that ebb and flow in their sex life.

For many others, it is still an unconscious but compelling force, just below acknowledged awareness, that drives their sexual desire. It is the aspect of their Eros that they have not looked at, or engaged in consciously. But during sex, in the moments right before orgasm, its true potency and authenticity cannot be denied. It completely takes over the body and voice in wild, fierce gestures, accompanied by profane, blasphemous invectives.

I believe those blasphemies, primitive groans and vocalizations expressed just before orgasm are often just a "sound byte" from one's PEM. The PEM is like a zip file, stored in the unconscious. It contains hours of content that includes all the elements of a mythic erotic story...archetypal personas, counterpart personas, setting, history, attire, dialogue, body language, props, et al. Some of these myths may stretch deep down into the instinctual layers of our psychological structures that stem from the mammalian (hot-blooded, alpha/beta pecking order – dominance and submission) levels of our inherent unconscious, and reptilian (cold-blooded, predator/prey – sadist/masochist) phases of our biological and psychological heritage.

These wilder, primitive aspects of human biology/psychology often show up in the myths, personas and physical expressions related to Fetish, Kink, and D/s-BDSM sexual expression. See Fetlife.com for a panoramic view of the full range of Fetish interests and the millions of people already participating in them.

While this is very early stage research, I believe this exploration into the psychological nature of Fetishsexuality could be relevant in regards to updating the outdated dating protocols still operating in the culture at large. People are still partnering and marrying without ever having discussed, let alone understand what each other's sexual desires look like, or how frequently or what kinds of sexual expression is central to their erotic nature. This leads to devastating erotic mismatches, which may devolve into all manner of shadowy, hidden, dangerous or deceptive behaviors eventually going on behind partners' backs, or shows up in other harmful ways that disrupt if not destroy the relationship.

People knowing their PEM and tools of how to communicate that honorably to a potential partner may be more apt to have a stronger bond in their overall relationship than not, as well as a fulfilled and well-expressed sexuality.

I believe that upwards of 15% of the population has an inherent fetish-driven sexual nature, held within a PEM(s), just as around 10% of the gene pool is gay or lesbian in their sexual orientation. I speculate that it may be a much higher percentage, and I am attempting to explore this theory further.

I devised the PEM survey in response to working with hundreds of my clients who sought to come to terms with their own kinky desires. In my private practice, clients came to me trying to understand this mildly to extremely kinky part of themselves that had been with them for decades in their fantasies, but seemed at odds with their everyday social or moral persona.

More significantly, it was often at odds with the judgments of others in their life, from their spouse, family, religious or moral views. This fear of other's judgment or discovery had generally kept my client's desire hidden beneath fear and shame. But these were life-long desires that never went away. This secrecy had led many to act out or pursue their desire in risky or unhealthy ways. Now finally they were coming to me just wanting to be who they were sexually and heal the shame fear and judgment that held them back.

The goal of this ongoing research is to help people with lifelong kink or fetish driven desires learn to embrace and express their authentic sexuality in conscious ways that are physically, emotionally and spiritually healthy, and in integrity with their values, agreements and intentions.

Though the research is preliminary, I believe that Fetishsexuality for some percentage of the gene pool is a life-long, inherent, innate sexual identity, on the same level that straight, bi, gay or lesbian is an authentic sexual identity, as defined by the American Psychological Association.

Some of the startling insights from over 2000 adults who have taken the PEM survey so far:

- *39% became aware of their sexual fantasies before age 10 and 70% by age 12.*
- *23% were masturbating to their fantasies before age 10 and 55% by age 12.*
- *40% masturbate to porn daily to several times per week.*

- *33% claimed their porn/masturbation activity led to more desire for their partners, 55% said it made no difference in their desire for their partner.*
- *54% struggle with shame and fear the judgment of others about their desires.*
- *75% claimed Dominance and submission was a prevalent aspect of their fantasies.*
- *Over 900 people voluntarily revealed very explicit and provocative snippets of dialogue common to their PEM while masturbating to their fantasies.*

About 51% of the respondents identified as female, 45% male, and 4% identified as other, such as pan-sexual, gender queer and a number of additional self-selected references. Respondents were primarily from populations that were already sex-positive in their views, not by random selection.

The 40 question, completely anonymous PEM survey, is a tool that helps the participant to begin to gain insights into the more specific nature of their sexual desire, particularly those in the more Kink or Fetish driven end of the scale. They can also begin to learn more clearly what resists or stands in the way of honest expression of their authentic desires. They can then begin to untangle the sex-negative unconscious resistances – judgment, fear and shame based internal messages embedded since childhood, from the authentic desire itself.

Here are just two of the many positive comments about the personal impact of the survey:

"I absolutely loved taking the survey. In life many look at sex as Taboo. Exploring your sexuality with your partner shouldn't be frowned upon. If anything you learn your likes and dislikes as well as his. Nothing is sexier that being the other's desire and exploring outside the realm of conformity."

"Thank you for giving me a place to try and explain what I feel. It is so nice knowing that I am not alone."

Those who take the survey are able to voluntarily opt-in to see the compiled results of over 2000 other participants.

If you are interested in reviewing or taking the survey go to: http://galenfous.com/pem.

This is YOUR life. I encourage you to be exactly who you are in all regards, consciously, humanely, consensually, erotically.

LOVE, ROMANCE AND KINK

A Conscious D/s-BDSM relationship structure offers a couple the potential to experience a range of love, romance, ecstasy and intimacy unleashed from the bonds of conventional norms. This necessitates cultivating a profound depth of trust, vulnerability and risk on both sides. If you and your partner seek an epic romantic, erotic adventurous love life, a Conscious D/s-BDSM relationship offers that potential in spades!

Whatever the Kink externalities may be for a relationship, there is also an implicit opportunity to reveal and share more of who we are at our depths. There can be the profound relief and gratitude of being accepted and welcomed at our darkest sexual edge rather than be shamed or judged. Supporting each other to feel honored and blessed for who we are, may also lead to feeling safe enough to express the ways we may have been wounded, shamed or made to fear our sexuality. We may be able to finally share our most hidden sexual desires, sacred and profane both that have been kept secret most of our lives. Arriving at this depth of honesty and trust with our partner can allow us to experience off the charts passion, love and sexual ecstasy.

When love and Kink are combined in an ongoing partnership, the complexity involved psychologically, emotionally, spiritually and physically goes far beyond the realm of egalitarian relationships and vanilla sex. Make no mistake, be it an occasional excursion or an extensive journey, Kink can be a very challenging relationship path.

Combining love and kink requires dedication, vulnerability, honesty and a personal commitment to the empowerment and heal-ing of both partners. In practice this means each partner is also do-ing his or her own personal work, in whatever way that makes sense. The intention of our personal work is to be more fully present, honest, personally responsible and authentic in the relationship.

This requires an understanding of one's counter-productive shadow behaviors (hidden, avoidant, shut-down or triggered) and the painful experiences about our sexuality, our worth, our lovability and more we may have experienced growing up. These are the experiences that led to our shadowy or protective behaviors being created in the first place.

Easier said than done. But if you embrace this path of relationship and work with it, it will ultimately be both an empowering and healing journey. And there is no guarantee it may not end in chaos, as can happen in any relationship style.

To smooth the journey a bit, here are a few of the key foundational principles I recommend to maximize love, trust, honesty and intimacy in the relationship and maximize ecstasy in the sexual realm.

First, there are no hard and fast rules for creating Conscious D/s-BDSM relationships, other than what two reasonable mature and responsible adults agree on.

Some couples may agree to include some level of Dominance/submission and Erotic BDSM as an occasional part of their sex life. For others it will be the context for all of their sexual relations, but not be part of their day-to-day life relationship. And there are those for whom the yearning for the power exchange aspect is so innate and instinctive that they "naturally" desire to extend these aspects into the ongoing day-to-day dynamics of the relationship itself.

D/s and BDSM are Distinct Aspects

One of the prime complexities that should be understood is the distinction between the Dominance and submission (D/s) and Erotic BDSM aspects of the relationship. While D/s and BDSM are intricately entwined, they are two distinct and inherently different dimensions as I view it. To better clarify that, here is the model I work from.

The D/s aspect pertains to the relationship itself and the negotiated power exchange dynamics that may be desired. These dynamics of D/s can apply to a one-time negotiated Erotic BDSM scene for an agreed upon period of time, or for committed couples, they can extend into the day-to-day relationship itself.

Through negotiated agreement, the Dominant has authority and control of the submissive in certain aspects of the relationship, or an individual scene. D/s does not in itself require there be an Erotic dimension, though there certainly can be.

In the right blend, the psychological foundations of conscious D/s power exchange can bring forth a noble, mythic, chivalrous quality to the relationship. The Dominant(as King/Queen archetype) can aspire to the highest standards of leadership, integrity, wisdom, responsibility, vision, blessing and other such qualities. The submissive (as devotee, servant) can aspire to service, surrender, seduction, selflessness, devotion obedience and more.

These are potent and beautiful qualities of character to reach for, that can inspire each individual and the relationship to a deeper dimension of soulful connection and profound love.

The mythic storylines and personas common to D/s dynamics have been part of human theater, the epic heroic tales of literature, and cultural cosmologies across the globe for thousands of years.

It is not just the physical sensations and sex that are compelling in D/s-BDSM. The regal status inherent in your psyche from your inner archetypal King/Queen met by the devotional surrender of your partner's inner servant or disciple, engages you both in an ancient psychic dance that can feel exhilarating.

For both partners, these ideal states are best considered aspirations, not destinations. They can be approached, enjoyed and experienced in ecstatic moments but cannot be perfectly maintained. Each partner is on a parallel journey that involves developing personal practices that support continually growing into the qualities of Dominant or submissive each one aspires to. This is a potent gift that each brings back to strengthen and deepen their consciously polarized relationship as Dominant and submissive.

A helpful practice in this regard is to learn how to engage in mindful communication with your partner. Set aside time periodically to review, adjust and fine-tune as you journey along the way. Let each partner speak freely, respectfully, and honestly about his or her feelings, concerns and desires, while the other actively listens. This is not a place to blame or disparage the other, even if a part of you is angry or "right!" Own your own feelings and judgments. Adjust your boundaries if need be. Allow any issue that may be presenting itself to be brought out, examined and mutually resolved. This is a place where the mythic dynamic of D/s should go to the background to allow any emotional, safety or logistical dissonance to be freely brought to resolution. This is the place for soul-to-soul communication to be the standard, rather than the D/s protocols.

There is no perfection in this. Allow yourself to expand into your chosen roles as Dominant or submissive in a way that is personal and meaningful to you both. It can become a lifelong journey of learning, deepening, healing and empowering each other and the relationship.

The Erotic BDSM aspect, on the other hand holds the shadowy sexual side of the relationship. It invites in all that is taboo, forbidden, inappropriate, wild, cruel, fierce, and more, that has been negotiated and agreed to. This is the realm of wild primitive beast sexuality – the hot-blooded mammalian alpha/beta territorial instincts, the dynamic of devouring, or being ravaged, and the cold-blooded predator/prey, sadist/masochist energies, all held within an ecstatic sexual engagement.

To explore these volatile desires in an empowering, consensual and erotically intoxicating manner requires the strong D/s foundation described above.

The agreements developed in the D/s realm create a safety net of sorts aimed to protect the soulful, loving, intimacy between each partner. This foundational rapport allows both to safely shine the light into the taboo, forbidden underworld of their sexuality. A couple can then explore their edgier desires in a pre-negotiated, well-paced way that does not traumatize the core body, heart and soul of each, while opening both to a profound wild erotic ecstasy.

At its best the engagement and connection of Dominant and

submissive in the realm of Erotic BDSM is a dance between the two polar shadow aspects of D/s. It is a dark exquisite tango. The sacred and profane become seamless and complementary like Yin/yang.

This is why it is very important to stay present and connected with your partner through all these levels so you may unleash the most fulfilling ecstasy available within the realms of D/s-BDSM Eros.

These may seem like risky energies to unleash, but with some conscious preparation, it is quite possible to create a negotiated path where these primitive Erotic energies can be safely revealed, explored, honored and expressed within a loving relationship. If these more intense edges of Eros are compelling and natural to your own sexuality, you can learn to explore them in ways that can be psychologically empowering and lead to off the charts orgasms and intoxicating erotic states of consciousness!

Know that over the last 20 or 30 years, millions if not tens of millions of people have successfully navigated and learned how to hold both sides of the D/s-BDSM relationship in noble and exquisite balance.

The essence of a D/s-BDSM engagement is a dance like the tango. Both partners are fully present and engaged, expressing authentically and joined as one. Each supports the other in reaching the deepest intimacy and ecstasy possible.

Paradox Expanded

D/s-BDSM relationships confront us with paradox on numerous levels. In the above distinctions between D/s and BDSM there is the paradox of the noble dimensions of the relationship with the ignoble exchange in the sexual realms. Understanding how to blend the sacred with the profane allows both dimensions to be fully expressed in a healthy, ecstatic manner. Creating D/s Protocols that include clear consent, negotiated boundaries, mutual respect, and heart to heart connection, allows our profane sexual desires to have a more safe and strong container to be held and expressed within.

Our generally neglected, secreted, Erotic BDSM sides really just want to be invited, encouraged, admired, respected and ultimately loved also! They are not intended to harm ourselves or our partners. They are integral and authentic parts of our whole selves. If kept hidden in shadow they will likely leak out into our lives in unhealthy, unfulfilling and often risky ways.

Many may also need to face a similar paradox within their own psyche. We have all been raised within a sex-negative culture that has forced many of us to keep our Kinky desires hidden from view. Most have a culturally embedded monotheistic judgment and morality that views our acts and desires as good or evil, civilized or primitive and right or wrong. It can be quite a stretch to come to terms with these paradoxes within our own unconscious psyches.

How can I be a loving parent, an active community member, advocate for human rights, a person of service, be a tender, loving, respectful and romantic man, and also be a dark-edged, sadistic, cruel, intense son of a bitch in the BDSM realms (Note: I can be tenderly cruel too!!). This requires an acceptance of the paradox.

Yes! I am both of these! One does not diminish the other. I can find ways to express my most profane, perverse taboo desires in a conscious, healthy, consensual way that is consistent with my values and moral and spiritual principles. How spectacular that both of these aspects of my soul are enthusiastically welcomed by my partner!

Many of us have been shamed and condemned about our sexuality and sex in general since we were children. Many have experienced being violated and traumatized. Even when we consciously choose to engage our desires and move past these shames, traumas and fears, they can still hold power over us and flood back into our beings when we do express our desires.

Some of these types of issues may require a deeper level of personal work to resolve. It might be best in some of these cases to work with a professional. But many issues from our past that might get triggered in a BDSM exchange can be shared by partners in a healthy way through vulnerable communication, compassionate listening, and being open to each other's histories and concerns in these regards.

This level of sharing and mutual care in itself can prove healing to each and build a deepening trust and intimacy to more readily embrace adventurous journeys into your wildest but authentic sexual desires.

Range of Protocol

In a 24/7 context maintaining some semblance of a total power exchange (TPE) is probably the most difficult and confusing aspect of a Dominant/submissive relationship structure. Most couples in this context will likely aspire to a very modest and flexible level of D/s in their relationship. Other primary life responsibilities for children, careers, employment, health and financial matters can leave little time for a formal everyday D/s structure. Most D/s couples will have very flexible protocols to fit into all the other realities adults face. But even if your goal is to be in a 24/7 Master/slave relationship this aspiration should also be looked at as a step-by-step journey towards that ideal.

Start slow and easy. Set modest protocols for a period of time, before advancing to a deeper structure. Do a periodic review that allows adjustment and refinement. Try to stay flexible and avoid rigidity. It is also critical for both partners to be clear about and hold their boundaries firmly. Due to the strenuous complexities involved, there are very few couples that will be able to maintain the extreme edge of a Total Power Exchange (TPE) D/s relationship.

It is in my experience impossible and impractical to totally be in control or give up total control in the complex real world. It is possible however to negotiate for what works for you in a D/s relationship, and to allow for renegotiation as you gain experience about what really is fulfilling and empowering versus drudgery or feeling exploited.

It is also possible to establish different levels of protocol peri-

111

odically as a way to strike a balance between one's deeper needs to control or surrender, and the ongoing practical nature of life. For instance you might establish certain weekends or other intervals as a time for high protocol, where requirements of dress, duties, use and service are pushed to more extreme edges of power exchange.

Then you can revert back to more relaxed protocols better suited to the stresses, strains and obligations of everyday reality. Again, I emphasize that this is a negotiated journey. In the conscious D/s – BDSM practices that I follow, both Dominant and submissive share equally in the negotiation of clearly stated, transparent agreements of their day-to-day protocols.

Stay in Touch

Some of the most powerful tools to maintain a strong D/s-BDSM relationship are embodiment and mindfulness practices. Embodiment means to be aware of and present at the body level.

We live in a very heady culture and are often in a disembodied state. When we are not very aware of being in our bodies, we are also not being present and attentive to the moment before us. Our minds are roaming constantly in the future or the past. We are barely aware we have a body at times. Using conscious touch, movement, breath and other mindful practices on your own and together with your partner can do a lot to shed the surface tensions of the day. These unconscious tensions can be disconnecting us, to one extent or another, from our heartfelt connection to our partner.

Sharing conscious touch, movement and breath together can enliven the body, activating the sensorial systems from head to toe. This will support being more present in the intention of the moment be it to have an important discussion about your relationship, or to step into the deep end of the BDSM pool. Developing and using these practices will help both partners feel more connected, intimate and freer to express their complex sexual natures.

Romance

Touch is the gateway to intimacy and connection. And beyond physical touch, you can also touch your partner with romance.

In this regard, I want to address the men. If you love and care for someone, romance can be easy. But most of us as men were raised in a culture where we lost touch. Lost touch with attentiveness, consideration, regard, respect, recognition, honoring, noting, blessing, gifting. If you think male Dominance is absent of any of these qualities you would be sadly mistaken. These are your strengths as a romantic Dominant lover. They are the most powerful of gestures you may offer to win trust, spark desire, enliven the soul, stimulate love and entice surrender. This is the power of the archetypal King of epic mythologies. The benevolent authority of your soul to bless, inspire and uplift the spirit of your submissive.

Being romantic should not be lost or neglected in a Dominant and submissive relationship any more than in any other relationship. I love to be my partner's lover and her Dominant. I want her to know and feel how loved she is. I do this by romancing her. Offering special gestures of my care, love and appreciation on a regular basis. You will need to find your own way in this regard, but let me offer some examples for reference.

Romance is old fashioned and ultimately timeless. Take the lead here. Even if the lead in this case feels clumsy or awkward, take a stretch into your own style of romance. Think in terms of making your gesture special. And special needn't require great effort or budget.

I send my partner surprise texts for her to awake to periodically. She rises for work much earlier than I do. Or during the day I send her a text just to say I love her, witness her, or thank her in some way or other. I let her know she is special, beautiful, valuable. I buy a bouquet of flowers for her for no particular reason. I reach for her hand when we walk together or put my arm around her. I look into her eyes when she speaks, and do my best to deeply listen. I encourage her truth. Wrap myself around her when I crawl into bed and pull her close.

She blesses me with similar gestures. Some mornings there is a tissue with a red kiss from her beautifully shaped lips on the counter next to my coffee cup. Or a sweet note, or a provocative flirtation in response to some vulgar suggestion I may have made. This is the tango of romantic Kink.

If you and your partner thrive on heavy degradation, humiliation and pain play in the Erotic-BDSM side of the relationship, the romantic loving interplay within your D/s relationship will be very important if not critical for keeping your submissive embraced in a protective core of your love, respect and regard for her ultimate humanity.

Time and Space

For any Erotic BDSM session, I recommend you set aside a minimum of 2 hours to immerse yourselves in these compelling personifications of your erotic nature. If this seems like a lot of time, you will soon find it might not be enough to take the full journey that may be waiting to unfold. You might find you could easily go 3 to 5 hours or more. Some scenes can be designed to go for an entire weekend or more. It is all about what you and your partner diligently negotiate and what your erotic imagination is compelled by.

Take care as well in preparing the space you will engage in. Bring in the ambiance of light, sound, texture, aromas and all that sets the right tone for the way in which you and your partner wish to journey. Make this a "sacred space", whatever that might mean to you so that it is as private, secure, safe and sacred feeling as you can make it.

Start with private time to prepare yourself. Engage in practices that help you get more present, clear in intention and embodied in whatever way works for you before you engage your partner. Close the computer, turn off the phone, do some conscious movement, mindfulness practices, breathe, let go of the day's tumult, and focus on your intention with your partner.

Take time to allow you and your partner to connect body to body, breath to breath, eye to eye and similar ways before you step into the Erotic BDSM scene you plan to engage in.

During the scene be mindful of staying connected through touch, eye contact and encouraging comments such as "good girl" that keep you both in the dance together. Maintaining this deep connection can allow you to bring an intensity and fierceness into your engagement that is mutually longed for. Without a strong continuous connection, bringing on intense predator actions, dialogue and pain could jar your partner into feeling disconnected, fearful or abandoned.

In any of these regards, when you are letting your inner sadist out, pay careful attention to pace. Start slow and build the energy of intensity a step at a time. Ease in and out of some peak level of intensity. Pay attention to your partner's body, breath and vocalizations. Move in and touch with a soothing gesture occasionally. If I am not sure where my partner is at in the course of some infliction, I will use a straightforward check in. "On a scale of 1 to 10, if 10 was Red (Stop), where are you at?" Each time you scene though, these parameters can change based on many factors that may be present in everyday life.

I am an Erotic Sadist. I can really enjoy being cruel, the Tyrant, the mindfucker, the abuser. I can enjoy inflicting pain of all sorts, but the intent is always Erotic. I have no yearning to hurt my partner if she is not at some level turned on by it. There has to be a compelling Erotic charge being exchanged. This is the place where the sexually charged personification of Dom/sub, in whatever manifestation it may take in the moment, has an opportunity to be fully embodied by each in an exquisite dance.

To maximize this potential I employ a technique called "sweetening the pain." I provide generous Erotic stimulation in intervals to keep my partner's Sex Creature happily engaged and on board for further intensity. This includes being aware of my partner's body and her particular erogenous zones be they, clitoral, g-spot, anal and numerous other locales. The sweetening aspect includes tender touch, encouragement and assurance at times, to let her know that despite where we are journeying we are still connected and entwined by the love and care we began with. This intermingling of pain and pleasure, cruelty and tenderness over the course of hours has most often led to out-of-this-world orgasms for both of us. But even without orgasm, this intense immersion into the depths of mythic Eros can lead to a profound intoxicating bliss.

All of these D/s-BDSM relationship tools can enhance your experience and support a deeper journey to unfold.

These guidelines are very broad-brush strokes depicting a highly complex and nuanced subject. They are elaborated on in other chapters to one extent or another as well. I hope they give you hints to explore these areas more deeply and find your own style and ways to explore D/s-BDSM in a conscious loving manner. It is an empowering experience to express your authentic self with an encouraging partner in all its manifestations, particularly sexually.

For me this experience has been the most profound feeling of being loved imaginable, and evoked my deepest sense of tenderness, care and love for my partner.

IS THE PROBLEM SEX/PORN ADDICTION OR SEXUAL DISHONESTY?
HOW TO GET HONEST ABOUT YOUR OWN SEXUAL NORM

There is a long unending stream of national news reports about politicians, teachers, religious leaders, entertainers, sports figures and other celebrities, caught in some variation of sexual dishonesty. Pundits and experts often label the behaviors, and the fall from grace that follows, the result of sex or porn addiction.

These highly publicized celebrity cases point to, but overlook a larger issue of rampant sexual dishonesty that is found at every level of the culture. These cases are just the visible tip of the iceberg of our collective sexual shadow, and the secretive ways we attempt to express our sexuality. Imagine all the rest of the population that are indulging their sexuality in covert ways. The stats are astronomical!

Based on keyword searches for affairs, visits to hook-up sites like Craigslist ads and Ashley Madison themed websites, not to mention all the secret porning by men and women both, our level of sexual secrecy and dishonesty is off the charts. Pornuhub.com a very popular adult pic and video portal reported about 1.7 million visitors per hour came to the site looking for porn last year. This is just one web site. The approximate number of unique visitors to all adult websites in 2006, per month, worldwide was 420 million! Pornhub single-handedly brought in that many visitors in 2013 in about 10 days!

Many people exploring and opening to their authentic sexual desires are inclined to keep their sexual explorations secret due to tangible fears of being shamed, harshly judged or punished about their personally meaningful and normal sexuality. Many take risks, in some cases very high risks, to express their sexual desires in dangerous clandestine rendezvous'. When caught in their infidelity, the sad, ruinous, mythic drama - the fall from grace, gets played out over and over, individual by individual, celebrity and not.

Many of these people get labeled as sex/porn addicts or self-label as addicts after the fact, when they are discovered. I believe in many cases, the often vilifying, porn/sex addiction label, branded or grasped, misses a deeper dysfunction. The significant issue being overlooked is what I identify as Sexual Authenticity Disorder – an extreme and often life-long effort to conceal aspects of ones sexuality and the fear of revealing or having your authentic sexuality discovered, shamed, judged or punished by others. The primary symptoms of Sexual Authenticity Disorder are intense fear of discovery, sexual secrecy, dishonesty, and an attendant shame and guilt.

You won't find Sexual Authenticity Disorder listed in the DSM-V manual, and this is unfortunate considering the pervasiveness of the problem, but neither will you find sex or porn addiction. Neither are currently recognized nor accepted as psychological disorders by the American Psychiatry Association, so my defining SAD outside APA sanction is not without precedent!

The reason people hide or are dishonest about their authentic sexual desires may fall within the sex or porn addiction model in some percentage of cases. Clearly excessive porn use can become a compulsive behavior. It may become problematic and lead to numerous imbalances in other parts of one's life. But is it any different than one's compulsion to check their Facebook feed, email, texts and all social media excessively. These compulsive behaviors do point to important underlying issues that are calling to be addressed, but I feel the excessive aspect is more the issue than what the behavior is focused on. If addiction is the model that makes sense to the one seeking support around their sexual expression, by all means, pursue therapy under the sex/porn-addiction model. But if the label does not seem to fit, even if you are a regular porn user or have a high sex drive, then consider that you may have not yet owned and honored what is sexually true for you. You have a right to be who you are sexually, and define your own norm in ways that are conscious, consensual and risk aware.

The sex/porn addiction model also falls far short of explaining the explosion of sexual activity awakening worldwide within a pervasively sex-negative cultural reality. It is clear to me, from the hundreds of men, women and couples I have worked with the last 14 years, and analysis of over 2000 people's responses on my *Discover Your Personal Erotic Myth Survey,* that these emerging sexual explorations are routinely conducted in clandestine, or secretive ways. My clients indicate this secrecy is due to fear of how partners, families, social, professional or spiritual communities may judge them, not because they are sexually addicted.

The narrow narrative predominant among sex/porn addiction theorists, the scandal driven news media, and sex-negative fundamentalists of every stripe, brushes over the emerging, explosive, ecstatic depths of human sexuality that are being explored and expressed globally, in a way that is unprecedented in the history of civilization.

My concern is that the current psychological tools used to assess someone as a sex/porn addict, a hypersexual or a sexual deviant, are inadequate and outdated. They do not allow for nor encourage this amazing range of emerging sexuality. Many assessed as having a sexual disorder may simply be men and women who have an alternative sexuality that is outside the range of those doing the assessment.

I am reminded of the poignant reply by sex researcher Alfred Kinsey when asked how someone can identify or diagnose a woman as a nymphomaniac. There was a similar over-the-top hysteria and handwringing about nymphomania in the 1950's as there is now about hypersexuality, sex and porn addiction. Kinsey framed it perfectly with his deadpanned quip, "A nymphomaniac is someone who has more sex than you do." In other words, Kinsey did not consider nymphomania a diagnosable psychological disorder. The implication by Kinsey was that normal sexuality should be considered as the personal sex-drive and style of the beholder.

The morally righteous, sex negative, inquisitional mentality that dominates the current cultural messaging around sex/porn addiction, is still focused on the control and repression of all but the narrowest range of sexual normalcy. For generations, the sex-negative messaging we have grown up with has created an internalized fear and shame that our sexual desire may be considered abnormal, sinful, sick or disgusting by the parent culture. There is a palpable fear that if revealed, our honest sexual expression may leave us outcasts from the ranks of decent citizens, and all the personal devastation that may bring with it.

These negative, judgmental, internal messages that many carry about their authentic sexual feelings, and the shame and fear of others judgment, has led to our cultural inability to be honest about our sexual desires. We have created a culture where sex is debased and pushed down below the surface. It is forbidden. It is unspeakable. We do not know how to talk with our partners about our sexual desires, to be honest about them, share, explore, or revel in them. We are supposed to aspire to be sexy on one hand of the cultural messaging and yet not look at others in a sexual way, or express our sexuality directly on the other.

The shadow of sexual dishonesty plays out just as relentlessly on our local and personal stages, as on the national. Partners cheating on their partners behind their back, secretly chasing after every perversity imaginable online or in real life, getting caught and having their lives thrown into tragedy, will be an ever increasing eventuality in the current sex-negative and dishonest cultural framework.

There is an implied sexual norm that we are judged by and expected to follow that is setting an impossible standard in this era of emerging sexual expression. What normal is, is never defined. Normal is…you know…normal! But there is a never-ending stream of opinion and even law about what is not normal. And if there is not a law there is a harsh fundamentalist social, religious or familial pressure, if not outright violence, to conform to this vague norm.

Any but the narrowest version of sexual authenticity can be and has been pathologized by institutional psychiatry/psychology and deemed a psychological disorder. This can and does lead to profound impacts in real world battles in divorces, parenting rights, employment and housing discrimination and many other areas of life. Witness the ongoing history of the gay and lesbian movements fight for their legal rights in all regards.

Contemporary sexuality is tangled up in outdated, archaic, and irrelevant moral and religious doctrines designed for a cultural mind-set equivalent to the medieval Dark Ages. It is my opinion that humanity has reached a point in evolution where our sexuality is busting loose from the ultimately flimsy bonds of fear driven moralities about the flesh, and our wilder, more instinctual dimensions of sexual behavior.

This fear about sex, and the fear about our partner or anyone else knowing the truth of our sexual desire, on the one hand, and the astronomical rise in sexual interest and desire clearly emerging in the culture on the other, are on a collision course. We can't be honest about our sexual desire, and we can't stop our sexual desire from acting out. This is a recipe for psycho-dramatic mayhem at all levels of American culture.

It is clear the cycle of people getting busted for secretively and dishonestly acting out their sexuality is turning faster and faster. This is a great tragedy that is due in good part to married and partnered couples being unable to communicate honestly about their sexual desires. The covert sexual shadow can only be overcome by an honesty of communication that begins before partnering, ideally, and carries on throughout the relationship in a negotiated way that acknowledges and honors the authentic desires and boundaries of each partner.

The key to coming to terms with our sexuality is to learn how to express and experience our desires safely, honorably and consciously, in a way that is in integrity with the agreements we make with ourselves and others, and that encompass our core values. We must also compassionately examine and resolve the unconscious but powerful sex-negative cultural messages, and real life traumas we've internalized about our sexuality and ourselves. This is why I believe aspiring to sexual authenticity is both an empowering and healing journey.

Moving the culture from where it is now, to a place where sexuality is a normalized part of our lives, openly talked about, learned about, embraced, and enjoyed is a monumental journey with no near term date of completion. But I am confident that it is the only path that can resolve the tremendous cost of our sexual dishonesty.

Healing Sexual Shame, Resolving Sexual Shadows

Most of the clients I have worked with have come to me in conflict. The conflict is between their hidden or inhibited sexual desire, and the internalized part(s) of their psyche that oppose the desire. They are stuck.

A fair percentage of my clients will have kept their desires a total secret from everyone, particularly if they involve Kink or Fetish. They will have had little to no real-time exploration as yet. Knowing how I hid my sexual truth the first 48 years of my life, I have the highest empathy for these clients. I am grateful for the honor of being the first person they have felt safe enough with, to share these well-guarded, but totally authentic and valid parts of their sexual soul.

Some clients *have* attempted some exploration, but with a noticeable, if not overwhelming sense of disconnection, shame or fear, following or even during the erotic engagement. They might describe having been in a mostly distracted, nervous state when they attempted to embody their desires. They express having felt clumsy or inadequate during sex, and feel that they have not gone as deep into their Eros as seemed possible. They can't fully feel themselves within their desire as they engage it. Something was still holding them back.

That something has a physical and an emotional component. The unconscious parts of us that resist or oppose our sexual desires also encumber us physically and emotionally. These thoughts and internal stories can diminish our ability to fully feel the powerful emotions and sensations of our sexual expression.

For example, one way my own inner conflict showed up was in a tightly clenched throat. In my late teens, when I first began to explore porn shops, I recall the chokehold on my larynx. If the clerk spoke to me, it took a herculean effort to squeeze some mumbled response past the vice grip around my throat. I also recall aversion of eyes, and heart leaping to the throat anytime someone entered the shop that might recognize me. It took a certain force of will to override these physical and emotional encumbrances that were hard-wired in my unconscious. I was often not up to the task of cloaking my anxiety about revealing my sexual desire when I was younger, and this only propelled me deeper into the fear and shame that was overwhelming my desire in those moments. As I got into the middle stage of my life, I finally began to learn techniques to begin to shed the physical and emotional power of these unconscious responses, so I could more completely express, and embody my true Eros.

I often point out to my clients how strong their desire has been, to survive the repressive and punitive assault it has been under for decades. I always find the resiliency and persistence of Eros quite amazing.

I have clients in their 40's or 50's who have secretly hidden their sexual desires since before puberty. Now cruising past middle age, the desire has not subsided nor diminished. In fact it is so strong that despite all the time it has been kept in a hidden underworld, chained in by judgment and fear, their desire is still quite alive. Clients know they want to, and need to cross the threshold they have been stuck at. But the staunch resistance of opposing forces in our psyche that judge or fear our sexual expression can become fiercer right when we are at the threshold ready to enter. It takes a lot of power to overcome this resistance. A fair number of clients tell me this fear was so strong they almost didn't come to their first appointment. I have people schedule and not show up, and are never heard from again.

I often do an initial phone interview before I agree to meet with someone. I am repeatedly reminded of the grip that had been on my own throat and voice as I listen to them struggle to talk honestly about what they desire. I am used to hearing, "sorry, I am really nervous, I've never shared these things before," to explain their difficulty speaking clearly.

This is indicative of the fear that so often heavily coats our sexual desire. It is a tragedy that mature, decent, intelligent people should feel so much shame and fear about their sexuality that they have to be so guarded. It is also tragic that there are so few places in our culture that know how to support and encourage anyone who simply wants to be honest about who he or she is sexually.

I had a new client recently who had asked for help in sorting out her secret sexual desires. On the phone, she could only hint at the sexual desires she had held back all her life. In a choked voice, she struggled to say that it had to do with "being taken." She wanted to be dominated. "This is so embarrassing to talk about." Some part of her was terrified that she had this desire at all. It totally went against her feminist and religious beliefs. But she was reaching a point where her erotic desire was overwhelming her fear and shame at revealing it. She knew something had to shift. We scheduled an initial appointment for a talk-only session.

On the way, she had pulled over and parked down the street. She was in a battle with every part of her that wanted her to turn around and run away. She felt like she might throw up. Her body and soul were shaking in fear, just at the thought of telling the truth about the nature of her sexual desire. She had never revealed it to anyone before. She was nearly 50 years old.

But she also knew she was at the point of no return. It was clear after all these years that her desire was not going away. Eros is such a relentless part of our being!

When she told me of her struggle just to arrive, I blessed her for her courage to confront and face the deep shame and fear she felt around her sexuality. Her story about the powerful urge to flee instead of show up drove it home for me once again:

It requires tremendous courage to overcome the deeply embedded fear and shame many of us carry around about our sexual truth.

I am struck by the high percentage of my clients who have told me similar stories about their struggle not to turn around on the way to their appointment.

How is it that such an integral, natural and vital part of who we are has become so vilified and repressed that we are compelled to hide it so desperately, and be so terrified of others knowing what our sexuality really looks like? Can it be anything but harmful to our physical, emotional and spiritual well-being to live in a culture where we are afraid to speak the truth about our sexuality? Our culture provides no place where people can go to feel safe, honored and encouraged to speak honestly about their erotic desires, at least those desires beyond the narrow range deemed appropriate by the conservative, sexually uptight mainstream.

It wasn't my intention to focus my practice on those who have never found a safe place, or someone they felt safe enough with, to reveal their most closely guarded sexual secrets. But somehow that has wound up being a good portion of my clients — those who reveal to me, for the first time ever, whatever sexual secrets they have held so guardedly, often for decades.

That is why I bless them for their amazing courage, just to show up! I am witnessing this Herculean effort by men and women who, despite their paralyzing fear, their overwhelming sense of guilt and shame, their bodies literally plunging into a state of flight, can still show up!

In this regard I am also struck by how deep, tenacious and relentless the soul of Eros is. Despite decades of intense repression, fear, shame, and vilification, Eros does not go away. My clients tell stories of how they have tried to forget about what they desire sexually, channeled it into eating, drinking, irritability, frigidity, spirituality or pornography. It did not matter! Eros was as strong a part of them as ever. Many had tried to keep their Eros locked in a secret world of fantasy and masturbation. They were all deathly afraid of getting caught, but still took huge risks in some cases to feed their desire in shadowy, unconscious or even dangerous ways.

I know exactly how my clients feel about revealing their sexual secrets. I came from the same place about 15 years ago. I had kept my interests in 'Fetish' and 'Kink' secret for my first 48 years, after a lifelong interest that began before puberty. I desperately hid it. I was so afraid of being judged, shamed or punished socially. My outer persona, or my perfect cover, was the altar boy, the Eagle Scout, the gentleman, the guy in the white hat. The leap to becoming sexually authentic was terrifying. I could not imagine any way I could have the courage to take the leap. An unexpected nudge from behind pushed me off the edge. It was a rough and tumble journey, but the blessings that came from being true to myself have forever enriched my life.

I am so grateful to be in a position now where I can offer the safety and trust that allows people to open up and speak their desire honestly. They can finally begin the process of learning about and sorting through the difficulties tangled up with their erotic desire.

Healing is a process of disengaging the fear, shame, harsh judgments, feelings of not being worthy and other challenges that have gotten embedded in the unconscious and that arise on cue, right along with our Eros. This tangled up expression leaves us frozen, or clumsy, or disconnected physically, emotionally and spiritually from the depth, power and exhilaration that is natural to our sexual expression. This is why the path to sexual authenticity is quite often a powerful healing journey as well.

In terms of moving past the internalized fears, shames and judgments that resist or stop our desires from expressing, I want to point out the relevance and significance of the body in these inner conflicts. Let's take the example of the restricted response in the throat when trying to speak about our sexual desire. The tension in the throat that strangles our effort to speak confidently is the physical analog of an unconscious conflict being played out internally. This inner mythic story portrays the conflict between the desire or truth of one's sexuality that is attempting to express, and the parts that are "choking" it back, literally and symbolically.

These unconscious stories portray the differing sides in the inner drama. There is always a major yes/no, hero/coward, good/evil scenario being enacted. In one's conflicted sexual mythos for ex-

127

ample, there is the truth of who you are – gay, straight, kinky, bi, or other, and embedded parts that oppose your desire as immoral, perverted, or a sin.

Your Erotic desire, when not distorted by the negative part of the mythos, is quite clear about what it wants. Your desire itself has no shame, and has a persona that can speak and enact quite naturally, what it wants. When your conscious self wants to voice your sexual desire, it has to do so physically. This is accomplished without conscious involvement through breath and movements of the muscles of the throat first, and then the adjacent muscles in the mouth, tongue and lips to make the words come out.

The opposing parts of your desire on the other hand, are doing their best to stop your desire from expressing, or from physically speaking. While these inner stories can generally be more elaborate, the core conflicting messages are what are significant. They can be thought as highly potent sound bites. "Your desire is pathetic. It's evil. What if someone finds out?" These messages being spoken in the unconscious psyche are, in effect, emotionally driven, and focus on generating as much fear, shame and confusion as possible to stop your desire from stepping into the conscious world.

These powerful negative emotions are expressed with corresponding muscular gestures attempting to suppress the vocal expression. In this regard, the effort to speak honestly about our sexuality is literally being choked by the muscular tensions applied to the throat and mouth's muscles by the conflicting embodiment occurring at the same time. This is the internalized shame, fear and judgment about one's desires, being reflected in the external physical body.

Up until now the client's Erotic truth has not been fully revealed or liberated from all that is tangled up with it physically, emotionally and morally. It is helpful to consider my client's desire, and these inner parts that oppose their desire, as two distinct personas.

The task at this stage is to begin to untangle the parts that resist your authentic desire, from the desire itself. In this tangled up state, the parts that oppose your conscious desire to fully express your sexuality, can and do dominate your desire. The fear and anxiety this opposing part generates has the power to force your desire into submission and withdrawal. Consequently, many people keep their sexual desire hidden and unexpressed, or express it in secret, shadowy, unhealthy ways.

This mythic internal battle between our sexual desires and their oppositions come together at a power point in the unconscious. This is the interface of the conflict. At this interface, there is, in a sense, or in fact, a mythic drama playing out. There are the opposing, righteous, moralistic, sex-negative, archetypal forces that convey their emotionally potent sound-byte messages. There are the archetypal personas of our desire and whatever defenders they may have mustered. Each side in the conflict is clamoring for power and control. The aspect with the stronger emotional potency will almost always win the day.

When we are mired in these internal conflicts, the tendency to act on our desire, or not, will generally lean in favor of the parts of us that oppose our desire. This opposing side is made up of harshly judgmental, fear and shamed based moral overlays embedded in our psyche from society, religion and family, and more directly, from mothers, fathers or other authority figures. These are routinely embedded in our unconscious during the social indoctrination of our childhood. The embedded conflicts described can feel especially overwhelming when someone has also experienced sexual violations, betrayal and loss of trust.

Included as well in our inner stories with similar structures and impacts may be self-image concerns: "*I am not sexy, desirable, attractive or worthy enough.*" Our inner conversation can also be consumed by an array of worst-case outcome concerns: "*What if my friends or family find out? No decent person would desire that. This will ruin my life. I will be humiliated and shamed forever. I am going to hell.*"

These are all potently charged, fear driven messages. They can have overwhelming power over your desire, but cannot conquer it.

In most cases of repression, Eros is just driven into a secret place, where it may begin to generate shadowy, risky behaviors of all sorts, or cause other problems.

The real power of these internalized fear driven messages is emotional, and therefore physical. The emotions can only be expressed through the body via physical gestures. These emotional and physical forces are much more potent than one's rational intellect. They are mythic in the sense that these messages are delivered in "character" within these inner stories. When we drill down into this level of our experience, there is observed more than just the message itself. It is also being delivered by a persona, with tone of voice, body language and other characteristics of someone who represents power over us. It is often the voice of the father or mother that we still carry inside. But it can take on many forms that have come from our experience or imagination.

Having witnessed or guided hundreds of people down into these aspects of who they are, uncovering, separating and fleshing out these distinct parts of themselves, I am quite confident that this model or map of the unconscious forces at play, can be applied to most anyone stuck in this type of conflict.

Fear is the most fundamental and powerful of these emotions. It was one of the earliest distinct emotions I believe. It first appeared in our reptilian past, when evolution hard-wired the instinctual fight or flight response. We carry basically the same survival hardware and software as our reptile relations in terms of fear and fight/flight response.

These sex-negative fear messages entangled with our desire are coming in on the survival frequency. They can cause the whole psychic and physical body to go into flight mode, anytime we get close to the edges of our Erotic wildlands. These opposing parts to our desire tell us it is way too scary out there. Too much is at risk. It is safer to stay in the bland repressed territory of acceptable behavior. These fearful parts are frantically screaming in some deep part of us, NO! NO! NO!

Until we can bring our awareness to the conscious and fierce intention to say YES! YES! YES!, to literally shout the NO down , the NO part will have the power, and the control over our desire. It will continue to exert its influence until we consciously choose to begin resolving it.

To begin to resolve these conflicts within my client's psyche, I utilize a variety of modalities. These include mindfulness, presence and embodiment practices, active imagine, symbolic and ritual practices, conscious touch and movement, straight-forward discussion, shadow work, voice dialogue and other methods, to draw out and externalize these conflicted parts from where they are bound up in the unconscious and in the body. Bringing the conflicted aspects into conscious awareness and teasing them apart can support someone to arrive at an empowered place of intention to choose what one wants, and diminish what resists one's intention.

There can be so much stored-up and accumulated stress in the body from the push-pull muscular tensions of the internal conflicts, it is often important to begin by working with the body. This is helpful to get someone in a more present state. Getting present means to shed as many of the irrelevant thoughts of the past or future not pertinent to their immediate intention. It means to be more conscious of the self-judgments and the internalized judgments of others, clamoring in our heads.

Getting present means feeling connected to, aware of, and at ease in one's body. To a great extent feeling disconnected from one's body or another's, derives from what I call surface tension. These are accumulated but minor charges of irritation, anxiety or melancholy and such that cloud our demeanor in the moment at hand. They also cloud our connection to being present in our body in that moment.

These surface tensions hold our body in certain levels of restraint as a result. A lot of this tension can be released through simple to learn movement techniques and breathing. This can help one to start feeling a greater sense of presence. Calming the body down through movement and conscious breath can help reduce the rush of thoughts clattering around in the mind. When we are captive to these thoughts, regrets about the past or fear about the future, we are generally disconnected from the feeling of being in our body, and in the present moment.

There are obviously significant traumas and experiences from our past and current life that may show up for us in a moment that are much deeper than what I described as surface tension. These would not be so easily shifted with the methods described. But a great majority of time the tensions we are experiencing in our body and mind are relatively trivial and quite dispensable.

From another view there are certain types of "armoring" that we protect ourselves with. This armoring happens in our inner psyche where we shield our secrets from view, but it occurs in the body as well. The body mirrors the shielding in our mind. This can be subtle when there is no imminent threat, but the protective expressions are always on-guard to some degree. The body stance may display arms folded over the chest, a slight leaning away from, little direct eye contact, a puffing or collapsing of the chest, or a certain overall rigidity. This physical defensiveness can also restrain our conversations with those we engage with. We keep the conversation at a more formal, sanitized intellectual level, telling facts and details rather than revealing the depths of what one truly feels in a moment.

Mutual touch and conscious movement with another can have amazing power to shape-shift a disconnected state of the body, to one more at ease and present. This can allow the mind to open and flow more readily. Often, when I get a sense of this disconnection during a session with a client, I will ask permission to hug, breathe with or do some movement together. Spanning that formal distance held between two bodies can build an intimate bridge that allows much that was unable to cross over previously, to flow.

The power for this more flowing exchange is coming directly from our bodies released tensions. The body itself can be experiencing a default sense of disconnection and low-level trust. Bridging this gap between bodies, through physical connection and movement, can sooth, enliven and disarm both bodies. The trust generated is now physical. This reorienting of the physical connection allows more freedom, depth, intimacy and creativity to be applied to the important intention the client wants to explore. All of these concepts can easily become practices utilized by any two people engaged in long term or any level of relationship.

Some of my clients come to a session out of an unmet desire for non-sexual, physical intimacy and touch, as much as they are there to resolve what is conflicted about their sexuality. Many of my women clients are specifically seeking to feel authentic, present, safe masculine touch.

We are coming from an era spanning the last 50 plus years where aspects of emerging liberation movements had the imperative of androgenizing the sexes. This is fine and good for those who choose to expand into androgynous identities and orientations. But too often men and women as equivalents, has been idealized as the desired state for all. This has discouraged the expression of personally innate masculinity and femininity that non-androgynous types desire to retain. As a result many het men in this era have lost or yielded their edge in their physical and emotional engagements with their partners.

These social and political ideological movements, despite being about liberation, can often hold a prudish, ultra-conservative shadow view of traditional heterosexual male and female relations. At the extremes, these liberation movements literally find themselves on the same ground as the patriarchal religious fundamentalists when it came to alternative sexuality such as consensual hetero male Dominance and submission and BDSM, the sex worker industry, pornography and sexual liberation generally.

This era has been important in opening the sexual landscape to welcome in the gay, lesbian, queer, poly, trans and other sexual identities, but it has been a confusing era for heterosexual relations.

To a certain extent this confusion created a whole new layer of tangles in the unconscious, in the relations between het men and women sexually, and in all layers of the relationship dynamic.

Het sexuality as well as sensual expression natural to an exchange between the het masculine and feminine to a great extent became confused and entangled with sexism, patriarchy, rape-culture and all such ideological constructs.

In my judgment, the distinct differences between the heterosexual masculine and feminine orientations are now ready to be more commonly and comfortably acknowledged and embraced, without diminishing in any way the newly established sexual orientations.

This 50-year emergence of androgynous and other non-binary orientations, while great for those ready to break binary limitations, has often left het men and women confused and disconnected physically, emotionally and spiritually from each other. On the up-side, the consciousness raised by the liberation movements allowed het partners to share a more evolved, respectful, egalitarian, harmony in their relationship.

This in itself was a good and necessary advancement in male and female relationships and attitudes. But there was a shadowy sex-negative edge, particularly against men's sexuality, that quenched the fires of many men's natural sexual passion.

Consequently many men's capacity for physical sexual engagement has often become progressively clumsy, passive and inept. I frequently get the complaint from women clients that their men partner's do not know how to touch them in a sensuous engaging manner, nor in the fierce way they longed for. Women client's also complained their men did not know how to stand up to them, to push back or at least hold their ground when they were out of line.

It is time to bridge these divides between het masculine and feminine expression in a conscious, empowered and mutually embodied way. But that can only begin by doing your own personal internal work to move to a post-blame POV.

THE BODY MIRRORS YOUR INNER STATE
PHYSICAL TENSIONS ARE AN ANALOG OF THE UNCONSCIOUS

Note: *This and the following chapter is based on an academic paper I submitted to a professional journal, so it has quotes and APA style references.*

This paper provides a synthesis of the literature concerning the duality of touch and talk between therapist and client in the psychotherapy setting. It discusses the ethical considerations, prohibitions, and attitudes about touch within the psychotherapeutic field. In addition, it looks at the client's perception of touch, types of touch, paradigms, rationales for the use of touch, religious and cultural considerations, the effects of touch, and research implications. Despite the reservations and lack of training around the use of touch in psychotherapy, there is a variety of literature to support its uses, benefits, effectiveness, and rationales, insomuch as there is a variety of literature about prohibitions, contraindications, and cautions of its use.

Many of us have lost a conscious appreciation for a fundamental part of our human experience…our bodies!

In other words, we are barely aware that we live in a body exquisitely sensitive, communicative, mobile, graceful, erotic, emotionally expressive and alive from head to toe. Our body's language reflects important information about our emotional and spiritual state.

In this chapter I hope to convey my own experience and insight about the relationship of the body to our emotions, unconscious psychological conflicts, embedded instinctual gestures, conscious movement, and presence. While this content is distinctly original, and has been formed out of my own direct experience, it is informed and supported by a variety of references, such as those noted throughout.

In our rationally based culture, we live to great extent from the neck up. In this heady state we are often in a whirl of thoughts, fears, judgments, stories, fantasies, shame, anger or sadness about the future or the past. We often forget to breathe and be still, to feel, to move, to be present.

Our bodies are often under severe stress and tension, mirroring the inner psychological stresses and tensions we experience consciously and unconsciously.

There are times we disconnect from our body altogether to avoid feeling a painful experience we may be undergoing emotionally.

This disconnection from feelings is like losing our psychological and spiritual moorings. "To lose our connection with the body is to become spiritually homeless. Without an anchor we float aimlessly, battered by the wind and waves of life." (Anodea, 1996, p. 54)

In already stressful times, additional tensions can be created in the body and psyche by our cultural imperative to soldier on, in a stoic manner, in what's considered a noble and responsible way. Until we break, or we break something else.

The body is an analog of our conscious and unconscious stress. We are either what we consciously embody, or what unconsciously embodies us.

Our emotions express through the body in specific, involuntary, instinctual, physical gestures. These physical gestures are choreographed from pre-programmed contractions or tensions of muscles and nerves. These physically encoded gestures show up subtly to overtly as frowns, tears, smiles, clenched fists, open arms, a knot in the throat and other involuntary movements. The body is an exact expression of what we are feeling, consciously and unconsciously.

All the fears, shames, angers and sorrows that our public persona tries to hide or repress, are still being expressed within the body. When we feel we have to hide our feelings, we are using opposing muscular tension to try to hold back the body's natural expression of the emotion.

The panorama of things that may be going on within us unconsciously, has a tremendous influence on the posture, tone and tension in the body at any given moment.

Most of us carry and are affected by negative stories, projections and self-judgments that are playing out routinely in our unconscious. These were mostly formed in childhood at critical junctures in our emotional and psychological development.

These unconscious beliefs about ourselves can generate strong emotions, when triggered by situations or other people that in some way represent that first trauma or emotional wounding. When we try to hide what we are feeling by "masking" them behind our external persona, our bodies store these withheld and hidden inner stories/beliefs/emotions as muscular tension in specific places in the body.

We learned in childhood how to cover up the feelings. We learned to "armor" our emotions and our bodies, to hide what we felt, and defend against discovery of what we truly felt.

We experienced that showing our feelings in certain situations could meet with disapproval, punishment and rejection, or for some, more severe consequences. Our efforts to hide or mask what we are feeling is a physical act. Tensions in the jaw, throat, shoulders, over the heart, the belly, can tell the same story as the tension-filled drama playing out in the unconscious. A common story many of my clients express bears the unconscious message…"I'm not good enough or smart enough or attractive enough or brave enough."

These negative self-judgments are alive in our bodies, as well as our unconscious. The body is the physical version of the story and the dark emotions we might feel about ourselves. The self-judgments show up in our body as tensions and discomfort, if not pain. Our bodies can be physically traumatized daily by our inner self-judgments. Accumulation of these tensions over many years may even bring the pain to disease level. Our bodies are fraught with disease – muscular, nervous system, bio-chemical tension.

This sensibility of the relation of the body to our unconscious stories and the physical, emotional pain or disease they can create, is finally being addressed by emerging somatic psychotherapy approaches to healing and health. In a recent study on the efficacy of the Rosen Method it is stated thusly,

"Bodily problems such as muscle tension are assumed to reflect unresolved emotional problems, suppressed traumatic experiences, or excessive social demands. The treatment focuses on the body, which is seen as a "gate" to reach unconscious emotional causes of muscular tension. A typical therapy session is set up in a calm environment and begins with a short conversation, during which the therapist pays particular attention to the client's voice, body posture, and movements." (Hoffren-Larson…, 2009, p. 996).

From birth, our bodies are encoded with hundreds of physical gestures to express what we are feeling in the emotional and unconscious aspects of our being. Smiling, frowning, crying, arms reaching out to be picked up, kicking our legs in anger, for example.

As we grow through these early stages of life, and experience emotional trauma or suffering, we develop a protective psychological armoring in an attempt to protect us from further trauma. This armoring happens in the unconscious realm where the emotional trauma (wound) and the protection strategy (shadow behavior) now reside. This armoring also happens in the body.

When we attempt to hide that we are afraid or anxious, sad, ashamed or angry, we are using counter muscular tensions and contractions to cover-up the instinctive gestures these emotions would normally express through the body. These counter muscular tensions are added to our unconscious physical gesture repertoire.

For example a small child's arms instinctively open wide as it runs to its mother when the child sees the mother enter the room. This is a programmed body language that is not taught. It is instinctive. It is fearless. It is joyful.

When a child's natural exuberant, physical joy is traumatized, or isn't met with a loving, safe response, it will begin to hold these joyful, open gestures back. The child's unconscious protections will physically restrain the natural opening of the arms, or smiling brightly. This requires muscular exertion from opposing muscle groups to create a counter force against the instinctual gestures.

Over time, we accumulate scores of these restraints and tensions in our bodies to protect ourselves emotionally. We unconsciously hide what is true emotionally, literally bury it in the body. The body, over decades, can become misshapen, rigid, muscularly armored, atrophied.

The physical and emotional aspects of our being are intimately connected. They are reflections of each other. The unconscious stores our judgmental projections about others and ourselves, and all the negative emotions associated with those judgments. It stores all the things about us that we hide or attempt to hide or deny about ourselves.

These internalized judgments can have a significant impact on our emotional and physical embodiment and well-being, in any given moment.

"It has long been understood that stress can cause the body to have physiological changes through the autonomic nervous system, the hypothalamic-pituitary pathway, the limbic system, the psycho-immunological response as well as other pathways that are currently being defined by researchers and theoreticians. It is logical to postulate therefore that anxiety and depression (or stress) will be important factors in the development of medical illness." (Kent & Blumenfield, 2011, p. 44).

Under acute distress, the emotions of unresolved fear, anger, sadness or shame can overwhelm the psychological and physical armor that hide them. The muscular ways we attempt to appear "normal" break down. Involuntarily, the body slumps, a foot taps rapidly, we avert our eyes, our throat tightens, stomach knots, we tear, blush, stiffen.

These physical gestures of our emotional truth, involve specific muscles, nerves and all sorts of bio-chemistry to express. Parts of us in our unconscious try to protect and preserve our public persona and cover up things we don't want others to know. This is done through counter muscular responses to hold back the true emotions the instinctual part of our unconscious is shaping our body into.

This generates tension in specific points in the body, where the emotion is being held back. The emotion literally gets stuck in the temporary stand-off between the "express" gesture and the "hide" gesture.

This is again reflected in the somatic, psychotherapeutic approaches such as the Rosen method.

> *"The therapist observes continually subtle changes in muscle tension, shifts in breathing, or other reactions, and responds to every change by touching the client or by responding verbally. During the process, hidden memories or emotions may come to mind, something that is assumed to provide valuable insights and assist the client in understanding the connection between body and mind."* (Hoffren-Larson…, 2009, p. 996).

Common tension points of stuck emotions, from my experience, are the shoulders, throat, jaw, neck, gut and over the heart. If we get to a place of extreme distress in the circumstances of our lives, the power of these stuck emotions, like a wall of water accumulating behind a dam, can burst through the unconscious "physical" efforts to block them.

In those moments, the body is flooded with this held back emotion and moves uncontrollably into the body's instinctive expression of the emotion. Under these circumstances, the gestures come out in an excessive outburst. We may "fly" into a rage, "flip out" of our reason, "break down" in tears," tremble" in fear, "shrink" in shame, or shut down, disconnect and fall into a catatonic depression.

These intense moments in our lives are often an explosion of a back-log of repressed emotion. They are released through exaggerated physical gestures. These explosions of emotion often have little to do with the immediate triggering event.

In the unconscious, our personal mythic stories are being played out. Many of our inner myths have a dark edge about the kind of person we REALLY are. The message of these types of inner myths can be generally demoralizing. It can leave us rooted in fear, shame, anger and sadness.

When we say we do not love ourselves, or feel we aren't loveable, there are actually a number of parts of ourselves that may be speaking in the unconscious. For instance, there could be an underlying sub-persona with a critical judgment about our lovability. This type of sub-persona can be telling us we are so messed up, nobody will ever find us loveable. And another wounded sub-persona agrees and says, "I am not loveable."

We choose so many conscious and unconscious destructive paths from this inner dynamic. We may stop caring for ourselves, and others, often in escalating ways. We may lose any sense of balance around everything from hygiene, dress, eating, smoking, drinking, drugging, cynicism, irritation, procrastination or other.

One healing pathway to help resolve the inner conflicts we experience is to begin inquiring more deeply into our unconscious beliefs, personal inner myths and repressed emotions that may be driving our experience and behavior. This is especially important if we find ourselves continually hovering near the extreme edges of our emotions.

Talk or cognitive/behavioral therapy may offer some intellectual insight and perspective. But the power of the emotional content of the internal issues we face are almost always more potent than our rational perspectives. Consequently, finding resolution of these types of tensions and conflicts may require exploring more emotion and body-centered approaches to healing core issues.

Some may find a spiritual pathway is the avenue to healing or resolution, as the issues may be understood not as social, psychological or physical, but as spiritual. But the spiritual view itself, depending on which one you may be influenced by, can inadvertently lead to a disconnection from the body as part of the spiritual belief itself. Contrast these two opposing spiritual views of the body:

141

"Disembodied spirituality is often based on an attempt to transcend, regulate, and/or transform embodied reality from the "higher" standpoint of consciousness and its values. Matter's experiential dimension as an imminent expression of the Mystery is generally ignored." (Ferrer, 1997, p. 8).

"This body is not me. These eyes are not me. It is a mistake to identify yourself with this life span, to imagine that you are separated from anything else in space or time. You are everything at the same time." (Lesser, 2005, p. 87).

I can say from my own experience that an embodied awareness is necessary for the full experience of life and even, at least while in this body, the sacred or spiritual realms as well. It may be possible through decades of intense meditation or such to achieve a disembodied transcendent experience of the divine. That really has no interest to me at all. I love the experience of being fully present in my body, and fully expressing my emotional being. This seems fundamental to the experience of life and perhaps critical to the long evolution of human consciousness.

Our nervous system seems hard-wired to integrate our body, our emotions and our consciousness. And the body in many ways stands on its own, as an integral but autonomous entity. Its consciousness is movement and action. It leads, follows, ducks, dodges, dances, threatens, charms, runs or cowers. It is primal. It shows fear, anger, sorrow, shame, love or joy without self-consciousness.

"As Jawer writes, 'without our feelings and their impulse toward expression, consciousness and intellect would not exist'. In Chap. 3, Jawer backtracks even further, exploring the neurobiology of feeling as the integration of brain, body, and self, associating the 'root of feeling' with the autonomic nervous system (ANS) and then moving up to the central nervous system and down to the enteric nervous system. What is significant here is his emphasis on the body as a single sensing and feeling organ: 'the bodymind, complex as it is, acts substantially as one'

"In other words, 'the body knows itself—it feels'" (Mayor, 2010, p 654).

A powerful "healing" pathway can be to work directly through the body's analog of an issue one is dealing with psychologically. While the emotionally charged, negative judgments we carry unconsciously about others and ourselves does shape the emotional and physical body, it is also possible to shift the emotions and the unconscious stories at any moment directly through work at the body level.

"The body is a dynamic unified complex system. All of its parts are interconnected and interdependent. Body and mind work together. They are mutually influential and interactive. This is called psycho-physical functioning, the combined interactions of body and mind. Because of this interconnected functioning, psychological issues affect the body and, conversely, the quality of physical interaction has an effect on psychological functioning." (Bowen, 2011).

More specifically through conscious movement, touch and stretching the body, we can literally "move" to a different state of mind by adopting a different body state, and therefore feeling state. Our emotions express through the body. If a client is "caved-in" from depression, supporting the client to open their arms out, expand their chest, or uplift their posture, can begin to have a similar effect on their state of being or embodiment.

Bringing touch and movement and other body centered practices into the realms of psychotherapy is still controversial and taboo in most regards. In professional massage and other body-centered practices, there are precise boundary protocols for hands on engagement of the client's body. However, most psychoanalytic practices that involve licensing have a taboo against the body and any touch between therapist and client. Despite the trust imbued to licensed massage professionals, the psychoanalytic profession cannot seem to untangle its fear that inherent sexual impulses will interfere with care for the patient. This separation of the body from conscious therapeutic efforts seems sadly out of date, if not "out of touch" with reality.

> *"Within the humanistic schools of psychotherapy, touch is generally an acceptable therapeutic intervention (see section on paradigms), whereas in the psychoanalytic movement, it is widely considered a taboo (Shaw, 2003). However, a gentle combination of both schools of thought has been conceived by some (Kupfermann & Smaldino, 1987; Winnicott, 1975). In taking into account the mind-body connection in therapy, some assert that literal touch itself is not always necessary for a "holding environment" (Slochower, 1996; Vitger, 1984), whereas others contend touch has, or may have, its place and value (Carere-Comes, 2007; Fuchs, 1975; Hunter & Struve, 1998a, 1998b; Kupfermann & Smaldino, 1987; Shaw, 2003; Smith, E. W. L. et al., 1998; Totton, 2003; Wilson, 1982; Woodmansey, 1988; Zur & Nordmarken, 2004). Others have strongly argued against physical touch (Burton & Heller, 1964; Wolberg, 1967). Classical Freudian analysts posit the sexual drive as the individual's primary motivating force and therefore link touch to sexuality (Gutheil & Gabbard, 1993)."* (Phelan, 2012, p. 98).

Developing a personal body-centered practice doesn't change the facts or circumstances of our life now, or our past. It does not heal or resolve by itself the deep wounding or trauma that may call for a deeper level of healing. But learning conscious breathing, movement, touch, stretching or yoga practices, in my experience, have the potential to shift our emotional/physical embodiment in a given moment. This may be enough of a shift to allow us to move from being trapped in our depression or lethargy, or irritation to be more present.

Being present means we are not in our heads in thoughts and emotions about the future or past, or distracted, distressed and unable to focus. We are more alive and grounded in our body, our breath, and at least leaning if not moving towards a state of joy or peace.

Many of the inner stories we get lost in or consumed by are about the short-term future or the past. There is often nothing that can be done "right now" to resolve what we are locked onto. Yet these relentless thoughts are consuming precious moments of our life. All the judgments, worry, anger, sadness we may be stuck in, are keeping us in a disconnected state. We are not at our best to look deeply at whatever the issues are, that are keeping us from being present. Nor are we able to enjoy, what may be a deliciously fulfilling moment that might be right in front of us.

To illustrate some aspects of how a movement practice can help shift attention away from being in one's head to a state of presence, I will give examples from a male client I have worked with.

R began seeing me to learn what was holding him back from the deep intimacy and physical connection he and his partner sought to have with each other.

He acknowledged that he felt terrible fear, shame and embarrassment about the awkward, unsyncopated movements in his body when he tried to intimately or sensuously touch, dance with or massage his partner.

In essence, he led with his fear, shame and embarrassment as his body state, rather than his masculine core. The masculine in dance or movement leads, advances and engages in a way that is compelling, but not bullying. The feminine follows. This is regard-less of biological gender.

From our earlier discussions, I learned how R was ridiculed, criticized and beaten down by his father, starting in early childhood. He wasn't "tough enough" or he was a "momma's boy". The father acted in the same critical, abusive manner towards R's mother as well. R developed a deep devotion to his mother in a number of conscious and unconscious ways. The experience of his father led him to make an internal vow to never treat his partners with anything that resembled anger. In fact he went out of his way to make sure he never "hurt" a woman by showing his anger.

R's relationships as an adult always revolved around him being like a sweet, anxious puppy around women. He had resolved as a boy to never treat a woman as his father had.

Additionally, the fear and unconscious belief he took in from his father that he was not good enough, strong enough, man enough or lovable enough, had manifested deeply in his body.

What he experienced in his unconscious beliefs showed up in his body. To a great extent he was not consciously "in" his body. He was unconsciously in his body and it reflected the fear at the core of his inner life through his timid awkward movements.

The goal was to help him get back in touch with his body. I put some music on, with a good soulful beat. I had R sit on the floor and begin by just connecting to the music, taking long slow breaths, while sitting still. I suggested he start from there and let his body move how it wanted to move, and see where it led. I gave him ten minutes alone to try to find what his body wanted to do uninhibitedly…to find his personal dance.

When I returned, R still sat on the floor. The music had a long slow groove. His arms were jabbing and punching the air in a herky-jerky motion with dozens of movements. He looked uncoordinated, gangly and out of rhythm. His head bobbed similarly. The rest of his body sat rigid.

I sat down back to back with R. At first, my intention was to use my body to guide R's body into a slow, smooth synchronization with the beat. This is not an uncommon theory of somatic body-work, that the therapist's body has a resonance with the client's that can synchronize in a way, to the clients.

> *"Body centered theorists often use the concept of somatic resonance in contrast to that of projective identification, underscoring the experience of therapeutic identification and somatic resourcing through the therapists bodily experience to more fully inform the therapists process within the evolving somatic dyad."* (Cornell, 2009, p. 78).

My effort back to back had no effect. R's body stayed steady in its off-beat dance. I then tried to "listen" to R's body, sitting still against R's back, letting his back muscles move mine in synch with his.

It was quite startling to feel the way his body was moving. I thought I might begin to feel some groove R's body was in. But all his movements felt random to me and not connected to the music. It was of course quite meaningful to him. But it was like weights, harnesses and restraints distorted his body's flow and hampered his organic movements.

I was witnessing, I believed, a shadow counterpart to the natural movement of the body as it dances its personal dance. I define the "personal dance" as how the body will move when it begins to shed years of stored tensions.

In the first stage of this "shadow dance" the movements burst from certain parts of the body like a tripped spring. Other parts of the body may still remain frozen solid, taking longer to thaw, if it is possible to move these parts at all.

For some people who have been severely disconnected from their body for decades, this shadow dance isn't capable of being on the beat, in rhythm or graceful. With some effort and a safe place to explore, the least encumbered parts of the body can begin to uncoil and release. Chunks of anger, fear, sorrow, and shame may come flying from the body in wild gestures.

With some intention and practice, these movements can begin to shift from unconscious, involuntary releases of physical tension to the conscious punching, swinging, jumping, shrinking, convul-sing aspects of anger or fear, sadness or shame they were expressing when first withheld. With practice, these movements can become more like a slow-paced release of numerous stored emotions and physical tensions.

In more extreme cases these highly wound inner tensions, when unresolved, may not be able to resist the explosive primal urges to blow our tops, punch the wall, slam our fist down on the table, shrink in shame, scream red-in-the-face invectives, or throw ourselves down on the bed in uncontrollable sobs.

Developing a practice to release these deep physical tensions in a healthy way, can allow us to be more present and grounded in our bodies.

MyYoga/OurYoga – A Personal Practice to Improve Presence and connection

About ten years ago I developed the conscious movement practice I use now, I call MyYoga.

MyYoga is personal. It is your own unique movements, guided by "listening" to your body as you move. Whenever you notice a strain in a part of the body as you move, you explore various additional movements that will begin to stretch, compress and release the tension in that spot.

MyYoga is related to the idea of the personal dance, but is more intentional in terms of helping you to be more focused on releasing muscular tension.

MyYoga is fluid. There are no pauses between postures you might explore and pass through. The flow of movement between each is seamless. Besides being an all-over tonification and conscious connection to the total body, it can work with precision when you locate a tension in some part of your body. MyYoga uses a wide range of self-directed movements and counter-movements, adding or subtracting parts of the body you are moving, and the speed, rotation, direction, torque and depth of the movements.

With the amazing number of parts of the body that can move, the infinite array of movements available, and adding that you can be standing, sitting, kneeling or laying down, you can learn to home-in on the precise movement and posture to reach even the most difficult places in the body where you feel tension. With some practice, you can start to release the tension in the muscles there. Recall these are not only strains in the muscle. They can also be stored emotions whose natural physical expression has been physically held back. Using MyYoga to start opening these channels can support emotional release as well.

You will know how and where to move by "listening" to your body. Listening means to be actively noticing what you feel in in your body as you move. This noticing guides you in where and how to move to interact with the tension in a way that feels "good."

Learning to be a good listener is a powerful act in itself in all levels of communication, besides in the practice of MyYoga. Listening is another high-impact tool for being more present in our life and relationships. By listening deeply and observing closely, we are disconnecting from the frenzied chatter and agenda of our ego-mind. Listening to another instead of already judging that we know what is being said, and focusing on our own response, allows us to remain more present and connected to the other person.

In MyYoga, as you move, keep all attention on "listening" to what you feel in your body. If you find your mind wandering off, come back to the intention to observe what you feel in your body, in any of the movements you are making. This focus on your body is rewarded with a conscious, stimulating, soothing connection to this amazing and significant part of your being.

Notice anywhere you feel something as you move. When you observe any strain or tension, experiment with that area. Slow the movement down, shorten strokes, rotations, go back and forth in and out of the strain, in smaller and smaller movements. You can further distill movements that stretch or compress the area. You can add counter-movements and torques with other parts of the body. Explore the area of tension further with micro movements. What decreases or increases the tension. What movements stretch or compress it further.

Just exploring your body this way is a powerful technique to allow deeper awareness and appreciation that you DO have a body. You can begin to sense how versatile, complex, expressive and informative your body can be, and how large a role it plays in your life. This felt sense of your relationship with your body is enlivening.

As best you can, never stop your movement during a MyYoga session. Let your movements be intuitive and spontaneous. You are not "thinking" about how to move, you are observing and feeling how your body wants to and can move. Movement makes the body come alive. And you begin to feel alive. Feeling alive means you are feeling your body. Moving to this state of being also opens you to feeling your emotions more honestly and authentically. You can begin moving past that stuck, disconnected feeling to one connected with your chosen intention and natural body-state of joy.

If you had been stuck in stories in your head beforehand that resulted in your body being in a state of worry, fear, sadness or anger, a movement practice can literally shift those feelings from within the body. In its place, you might find your body will have moved on to a state that is more calm, less tense, and your awareness will contain less worry and doubt. You may start to become aware of the feeling of being grounded or more deeply connected to your body. This is the state of presence, as I define it. This is the state where unresolved or stirred up aspects of the unconscious are no longer dominating the feeling or emotional state, nor the shape of the body in the moment. From here, one's conscious awareness, intention for the moment, the body, and the unconscious can be in better alignment and harmony with the ever-present moment of now.

References

Anodea, J. (1996). *Eastern body, western mind*, Berkeley, CA, Celestial Arts Publishing.

Bowen, B. (2011). Psycho-physical therapy, n.d, para.3, retrieved http://www.psychophysicaltherapy.com/ppt/whythebody.ht ml

Cornell, W. F. (Apr-Jun, 2009). Stranger to desire: Entering the erotic field. *Studies in Gender and Sexuality, 10*, 78.

Ferrer, J. N. (2008). What Does It Mean to Live a Fully Embodied Spiritual Life? *The International Journal of Transpersonal Studies, 27*, 1-11.

Hoffren-Larsson, R., Gustafsson, B., & Falkenberg, T. (2009). Rosen Method Bodywork: an exploratory study of an uncharted complementary therapy. *The Journal of Alternative and Complementary Medicine, 15*(9), 995-1000.

Kent, L. K., & Blumenfield, M. (2011). Psychodynamic Psychiatry in the General Medical Setting. *Journal of the American Academy of Psychoanalysis and Dynamic Psychiatry, 39*(1), 41-62.

Lesser, E. (2005*). Broken open: How difficult times can help us grow.* New York, NY, Villard Books.

Mayor, D. F. (2010). The Spiritual Anatomy of Emotion: How Feelings Link the Brain, the Body, and the Sixth Sense. *Journal of Religion and Health, 49*(4), 653-656.

Phelan, J. E. (2009). Exploring the use of touch in the psychotherapeutic setting: A phenomenological review. *Psychotherapy: Theory, Research, Practice, Training, 46*(1), 97-111.

INTEGRATING YOUR SEXUAL AND PUBLIC PERSONA

No matter how much psychological, emotional and spiritual work you do to be empowered, resolve shame and find inner harmony around your sexuality, you will still be faced with how you present yourself to partners, family, friends, church members, and work relationships, not to mention your kids.

Ultimately it is entirely personal how you dance the edges in being true to who you are. You have a right to your privacy. You have every right to side-step energy draining, pointless inquisitions from sex-negative ideologues of every stripe that you do not give one shit about.

It reflects the pathetic state of personal freedom across the world that anyone has to consider how others may judge their sexual identity and preferences. But there are serious consequences that could result from those with some influence and power over us, who might view our sexuality through a sex-negative lens. This can include those within the realm of our primary and family relationships, our employment or professional life, our academic tracks, and all across the social, spiritual, political and legal spectrum. There is no easy path here. It is very complex terrain, and will be uniquely complex for each person. It can be a challenge to enjoy the ecstatic freedom of your liberated sexuality and also be wise in how, when, where and to whom you come out.

For many of us this is a challenge that can come up on a daily basis, depending on what other areas of our life we are active in. It may not come up overtly, but there can be very powerful and disturbing undercurrents provoking our psyche in some of the highly political or religious environments we may naturally operate in. In this context we can be faced with situations where what is true for us sexually may be grounds for dismissal from employment, loss of relationships or vilification, public shaming and ruin.

I have often been forced to dance on this delicate edge over the last 15 years. There are several areas of my life as a father, an entrepreneur, a business consultant, workshop leader and mentor to teen boys that have brought this dilemma into uncomfortable focus.

I have never backed away from my sexual lifestyle as an integral part of who I am, but in many situations, I do not bring it into the conversation. This omission would be in contexts where an inopportune revelation could make life extremely complicated or lead to loss of business, friendships or other social connections that may otherwise have value. In other contexts, it is entirely irrelevant and frankly nobody else's business what my sexuality looks like.

Needless to say, part of me has been very wary to expose myself to the vitriol of strangers who want to protest my sexual preferences, if not outright condemn them, and myself as well. Been there, done that! I now take a "choose my battles" approach. No sense wasting precious life-force pointlessly debating people who are not a relevant part of my life.

But whenever it is brought up, which can happen easily enough in my case, by Googling my name, or cell phone number, I always tell the truth, no matter the outcome. It is an incredibly liberating feeling to know I will no longer hide who I am, and not care who knows it, as my bottom line.

Initially, I did not realize how this choice of nondisclosure was also fracturing my psyche at times. My choice to be discreet, or be concerned about revealing my personal sexuality and my professsional work, seemed a practical effort. I was simply choosing to not complicate and jeopardize other unrelated business I was developing. But I eventually realized this nondisclosure could generate a subtle inner shame or shrinking in my spirit, the same as if I was hiding some horrible secret that I feared would be dis-covered. This subtle but deep sense of internal shaming was important to get to the surface.

I came to this realization about 10 years ago when I was in the midst of negotiating a deal with a company called Pro Performance Sports. They were interested in a distribution license for a baseball/

softball glove design I had patented that was originally licensed to Rawlings Sporting Goods.

The company was really excited about the opportunity to re-license my innovative glove design, and were flying me down to San Diego and hosting me rather lavishly to put a deal together.

The night before I was to leave, I did a meditation at my personal altar to prepare for my negotiation with them. I noted how excited a part of me was to be sought after in an all-expenses paid manner. I felt the pleasurable sense of having the upper hand. But I also noticed this physical and emotional disturbance…a discomfort in my gut. As I observed more, I became aware of this huge, but unconscious anxiety around them discovering my work in the nether regions of sexual perversity!

I noticed a part of me wishing I had used my middle name instead of my first name in my correspondence with them. What if they Googled my name and found my Tetruss and my pro Dom sites or my book. I had also mentioned this trip to my teenage sons, and felt another undercurrent of my anxiety. What if they mentioned it to their mom, who had made numerous attempts to slander me with ruinous intent, since a bitter divorce 5 years earlier. Part of me was feeling paranoid she was going to sabotage the deal by calling them and outing me as a pathological pervert. She had done similar violations in the years since our divorce. She viewed my Kink sexuality like I was a child molester…or less!

I was struggling financially at that moment and getting the advance they had dangled in front of me felt like a luxurious life preserver.

I became aware of how very fearful this part of me was feeling about this trip. I could now start to hear messages of shame coming from the inner voices of my paranoia. "They are going to Google my name for sure. They will think I am a fucked up sexual deviant. I could jeopardize their business if they got into a deal with me. My sexuality is dangerous to others I associate with. I am not an acceptable partner."

155

Ever since getting outed and being caste out from my previous vanilla community during my divorce, I have carried some sub-conscious sense that my Fetish identity exposed others I associated with to the same judgments and condemnation I had suffered. The message was, I am poisonous, and if exposed to others, deadly. It was a subtle but very deep fear, an inescapable dread that this inner horror story might become true.

This moment of meditation before my altar brought a powerful realization to my awareness. The very parts of my sexuality I had worked so hard to embrace and honor, to call up out of hiding and shame, were now being shamed and judged by other unresolved parts within myself. I was stunned to finally see this inner conflict. I was giving away my power to this fear. Part of me wanted to hide or cover up my authentic identity. I was being kept off-balance by the unresolved turmoil of this inner conflict. With this deep revelation, I was inspired to create a ritual that evening to embrace all of me.

I stood before my personal altar and took in all the sacred objects, symbols, mementos and other artifacts that were an externalized representation of the many aspects of my entire self. I believe an altar is like a psychic recharging station. It stores potent symbols that resonate with and reflect back to me what is within my self already. To be effective, I believe an altar should only hold symbols that are personally meaningful. Each artifact on my altar that evening represented something inside of me that was personally meaningful and important – my fatherhood to my sons, people who I have journeyed through life with, people I love and who love me, powerful experiences I have had, values and goals I aspire to, and my life's milestones and actions I have taken in the world related to my mission.

This later aspect included artifacts relating to my first book, The Sharp Edge of Love, the Tetruss suspension bondage rig, my pro Dom work, and numerous other artifacts of my Kink lifestyle. ALL of me was unabashedly on display upon my altar. Nothing was hidden! There was nothing to hide.

I suddenly felt the celebration that should be going on within me, especially around my sexual liberation and mission, rather than shame and fear. ALL of me, is who I am! Fuck hiding any part of me that is true. I realized I really am quite proud of my sexual journey. I am NOT this old pattern that wanted me to be afraid and ashamed. This ritual helped restore my sense of wholeness and brought a sense of empowerment back into my body, emotions and spirit. I was still in the place to choose who and how I might share that aspect of me. And I released any fear that my sexual authenticity could sabotage this deal or my life.

It is your right to find your own path and pace of how you come out and to whom. Be as discrete as you feel is right for you. Do whatever type of personal work to empower and heal around your sexuality that works for you. Your sexuality is your birthright. I encourage you to feel proud of who you are sexually and shed all the shame and fear it may be tangled in. When you are ready, start connecting with emerging sex-positive communities that will welcome you and encourage you as the sexual being you are. Or just keep it between you and that special partner you share it with. It is your right to choose your own path.

THE NEXT STEPS

For Singles…

If you are single, you might approach your dating process in a new way.

If you have decided to finally include your sexuality in your life as if it were normal, and more significantly, as vitally important, you will want to honor that, and be clear about it with your potential partners. If you are really grounded and clear about what you desire, you might stay within your usual territory for finding dates, and make an intention to initiate a discussion of what your desires look like…before the first date ends!

Usually on a first date, in the vanilla world, you are exploring many important areas with potential partners. The whole idea is to get to know each other's compatibility. Are they single or partnered? Are they looking for a long-term partnership, or more casual? Are they local, just visiting, or moving soon? Do they have a job/career/children? What are their religious beliefs and more?

Now, with your new-found intention to find a partner who you can be yourself with in all your sexual glory, why would you want to wait, or find out later down the path your new prospect shares no interest at all in your desires. They may have potential to become good friends, but offer zip in the Erotic zone and consequently a long-term relationship.

Speaking openly and directly about your sexual preferences is going to be a huge stretch for many people to apply in their conventional dating territory. In the pervasive vanilla dating world, the old, ancient and outdated traditions still prevail. Even with the growth of egalitarianism over the last 50 years, certain protocols in the vanilla dating realms often expect guys to initiate and pony up for dates, if they want to be taken seriously. There can be expectations to present other material symbols of affection, throughout an indefinite and protracted dating period. Renaissance era chivalry and virginal sweetness, sans hot sexual need, are expected to be in the lead.

For many you would meet in the vanilla dating world, expecting or offering more than a kiss on the first date, would be considered being too forward. Initiating a conversion about sexual desires and experience levels upon first meeting may lead to you being considered uncouth, uncivilized, dangerous, a sex-fiend, sick or other such judgments. Of course, if they pronounce such judgments with a big smile of approval on their blushing face, you may have un-covered a kindred soul.

If asking your date to have a mature, informational discussion about their sexuality, feels near impossible in the vanilla dating world you have roamed in, I suggest you enter a different world.

If you are serious about embracing your fundamental right to express your sexual truth, there are more straightforward paths to finding dates or potential partners that are open to your desires.

There are all kinds of dating sites and apps that offer the full range of available erotic singles or polyamorous types, from the sacred to the profane ranges of Eros. There are meet-up groups, lifestyle events, socials or munches, workshops, play-parties, snuggle parties, and erotic guides of every stripe to help you take those first steps in your journey.

Seeking out and exploring these sexually open communities is a ready way to immerse yourself in a population of others who are on a similar path of exploration. These are also the places to learn more about cultivating personal practices that lead to greater presence, embodiment, mindfulness, negotiation skills, consent, honesty and integrity.

All of the legitimate sex-positive groups you uncover, will offer friendly ways to be introduced to their events, and do not require hands-on participation to check out the group. Most will have sensible rules published and enforced at events for the safety of all, offer safe-sex supplies if sex is part of the event, and frankly, go out of their way to make their events feel "normal" and welcoming, as off-beat or freaky as the group may be.

Many people, understandably, will not feel in a position, due to their public personas, to participate above the radar. For those who feel the need for privacy and discretion in exploring their sexuality, there are a number of popular adult dating sites and phone apps, easily found in the search engines. There are a lot of people who successfully connect this way, and keep their desires private in the rest of their life.

Online dating can certainly be a very frustrating and time-consuming experience. Women in particular can be bombarded with replies to a dating profile ad, moments after it goes up. Most sites will have filters that will dump a good number of irrelevant replies. Many of the responses people receive or ads responded to will have some level of insincerity, immaturity or dishonesty embedded, be they from men or women. People can purport to be anybody they care to make up on the Internet, and an unfortunately high percent-age will be completely insincere.

Torrid email or text exchanges can lead one to believe they have met their soul mate, or the hottest fantasy they have ever dreamed of.

But, how do you know the person you read on the screen is who they say they are?

Let me offer some guidelines I have used successfully from my own on-line dating days.

Whatever responses the filters you place don't catch, delete all one or two sentence replies, unless it sounds like a Shakespearian couplet! If you requested a photo, and there is none, for no good reason…gone. If they don't give straight-forward answers to straight-forward questions…delete. If after a few emails, they are not willing to Skype or meet in a public place for coffee or such…gone!

As I said, the online dating process can be very time consuming. I know that no matter how compelling the connection may feel in email/text exchanges, nothing is really known until I meet someone in the flesh. If on meeting, it turns out there is no real connection, for whatever reason, it would have been regrettable to have spent months online exchanging futile emails.

In my experience it is imperative to explore and verify your desires. Having a compelling fantasy is great, but does it translate into fulfilling, real time expression with a consenting partner? You won't know this for a fact, before exploring in real time. And even then you may get confusing signals about your own desire, if you and your new partner are not on the same page sexually.

I do not mean for it to sound so complicated to be and express who you are sexually, but the truth is, that in most regards our sexuality is a highly complex, paradoxical aspect of who we are. You can only know your sexual self and your partners by taking the journey into the unexplored sexual wilderness. Like any journey into wild uncharted territory, be prepared!

If your goal is to find a long-term partnership that includes your particular sexuality, frequency of engagement and all such parameters, then it will be very important to experiment with your potential mate to get a better or confirmed sense of your mutual compatibility. Hoping to experiment and explore along the way with someone you already have committed to, offers a very low percentage chance of finding sexual harmony.

To come to the fullest knowledge about your sexuality, it might be sensible to indulge in explorations where commitment and long-term relationships are not necessarily part of the equation. This is your laboratory. It is the place to experiment, explore and get to the truth of what your desires are.

Be responsible for your own safety emotionally and physically. Do due diligence on potential partners. Trust your instincts. Take proper precautions. Stay within your comfort zone at the start and change the pace of engagement, only as it feels right. But I encourage you to find a path that allows you to explore and experience what you desire, as the best preparation to pursuing a long-term Kink relationship.

Personally, I would more prefer a partner who already had a depth of exploration behind them, versus someone who has some fantasies they think they might like to try. Eros is like a very intimate and passionate dance. It takes two to tango! If you are already a good dancer, you are likely more compelled by partners who dance well, much more than a novice. If you are just beginning, practice, practice, practice, learn, explore and grow to be best prepared for when your dream partner may show up. If you are still clinging to the story that you need to wait to have sex until you are committed or married, then you are facing a steep uphill journey on the path to sexual fulfillment.

The next steps if you are married or partnered and not sexually compatible…

For those already married or partnered, what do you do if there is just no way that your partner can share your sexual desires? Of course this won't be known definitively if you both have not had an honest discussion about your desires, and then an exploration.

It is possible that in the history of your relationship, negative glimpses of what your partner's response might be, have bled through the veil that shrouds and protects your hidden desires. Your understanding of their potential disapproval may have come from direct experience. Or it may have come through an unrelated third-party event.

On the male side of this equation, maybe your partner has related how so-and-so's spouse, part of your couple's circle, discovered he was visiting web sites depicting Female Domination. Your spouse relays the story with thorough disgust at this man's sick desires. His sneaking behind his partner's back. His infidelity. The risk of AIDS is brought in. Your friend's wife has demanded he get psychological or spiritual counseling to fix his immoral or sinful abnormalities, or his porn addiction, even if he did nothing more than view Femdom porn a few times online.

Imagine you just happen to have the same proclivities, and have viewed similar sites, as your male friend. This well-hidden part of you, may just be tingling in fear right about then *("Did I clear all my browser history?")*. Soon the conversation with your spouse gets to the interrogation round. "You wouldn't visit a web site like that would you? Have you? You're telling me the truth, aren't you?"

Or worse, maybe your partner HAS uncovered hints or more of your own proclivities, and has made it quite clear about their abhorrence of your desires and fantasies. Your partner assumes the moral high-ground and threatens to shame you further if your desire ever shows up again.

When your partner has made it clear that your desire is unwelcome, if not found abhorrent, or even pathological and dangerous, what do you do with your Eros?

The options are clear but difficult. You could justifiably conclude you and your partner are fundamentally incompatible sexually and leave the relationship. A simple solution, but of course highly complex in practice to untangle the emotional, financial, social, family and spiritual bonds involved in a long term relationship.

If you choose to stay in your relationship without doing anything about the imbalance sexually, you are faced with staying in the same shadowy, secret patterns and frustrations you have had throughout the course of the relationship. You will still face the risk and fear of exposure, if you pursue your desire in a secretive manner, and still have to face the disturbing consequences that may bring. You could choose to bury your desire, banish it from your attention. This will simply transform Eros into the demon it can become when denied. It will rebel. The rebellion may transform Erotic energy into neurotic energy - overeating, irritability, substance abuse, compulsive porning, faux-spirituality, or other health, psychological and relationship problems.

Under these circumstances it may be best to seek out someone in the helping professions who can facilitate a frank discussion with your partner. The goal is to find a way that allows you to be honest with your partner, negotiate new agreements that do not dishonor your very essential sexuality, and allows you to remain in relationship.

It is unfortunate there are so few competent resources in the relationship counseling field, that are experienced in supporting couples through the more far ranging aspects of sexuality. Most traditional relationship therapists are uninitiated in helping couples honor exactly who each partner is sexually. These important skills are generally not considered nor taught in academic psychology courses. If you seek counseling, a good resource to check out is the *National Coalition for Sexual Freedom* website. They host a list of local and national Kink Aware Professionals who may be better suited to your needs.

If they have the requisite skills, a good facilitator may offer even-handed support so that both sides can speak honestly about their sexuality and their concerns no matter the nature of one's sexual desires. This facilitated approach may help the couple better understand what may be different between them sexually. They could learn to develop realistic compromises and equitably re-negotiated agreements. They could learn to cultivate a vulnerable honesty that allows for deep trust and intimacy to form, and especially for ways each can honor and fulfill their sexual truths, without threatening the relationship.

However it occurs, the best course of action to preserve your relationship from this point is to have an open discussion on how the relationship can include sexual honesty going forward. This discussion should include an honest expression of what sexual desire looks like for each of you, as well as a clear definition of what desires would be outside each one's capacity. In other words, you would both negotiate your boundaries. Both would also talk about what they might fear about the other's desire, and also what might turn them on about it.

Undertaking this level of discussion is clearly a stretch for many people. It may seem impossible to consider having such a vulnerable conversation with your partner. Deciding to talk about sex, when it has never really been talked about in a long-term relationship, can have the potential to be treacherous, jagged and volatile. The intended conversation could potentially spin out of control into hurt or shut down feelings, anger, harsh judgment, projections, mistrust and disconnection.

But an honest discussion about sex can also be a path to deeper intimacy. In some cases it may be the only path left to preserve an otherwise fulfilling relationship. This is why it can be important to have the support of a sex-positive facilitator to help you both through this complex terrain.

For better or for worse, the majority of us at this stage of emergent sexuality will often be forced to be the pioneers of sexual honesty. The unchartered territory of our deepest erotic desires has few road maps, books or guides to follow. We are just at the beginning stages of understanding how to resolve and untangle what may be decades of fear, shame, confusion, antiquated morality, trauma and the vilification of sex. These entanglements encumber our efforts to arrive at the alluring oasis of intimacy, trust, honesty, deep connection and the wild perverse sexual ecstasy that we seek with our partners.

If you do choose to stay in a relationship where your sexual yearnings will never be welcome, what might you do?

Ask yourself; does my sexuality have a fundamental right to be part of who I am? Is it important, valid, authentic and integral to whom I am? Would I be a better, happier, more at-ease partner to my mate, if my sexuality were given more allowance and recognition – even outside the relationship?

Until a few years back, I had judgments about single or unencumbered people engaging in secret affairs with others who were already married or partnered. I had the same judgments about the married party as well. It was one thing for a partnership to crumble from within, but for it to happen due to a "home-wrecker" scenario, seemed a violation of trust and honesty beyond my limit. I still hold this true in almost all regards. I would not knowingly engage myself or support others in the pursuit of someone who was already partnered, or vice-versa, unless they had their partner's knowledge and encouragement. Honesty and trust are, of course, the foundation of a successful relationship.

But over the years I have found it clear that there are conditions in many relationships that puts one partner in a position of having to deny, repress, or abandon their own passions, and in some cases any physical affection at all. This, I believe, is grossly unfair to the denied partner. I cannot reconcile anyone's sexual passion being made so insignificant that it does not merit any accommodation in a relationship.

This is why I feel honest communication at the beginning of the relationship is so important. If it was made clear in advance of committing to someone, that our potential partner's boundaries, desires and frequency of sexual expression were so different from our own, we would likely decline the relationship. This assumes one is committed to including sexuality as an integral part of their relationships.

About 12 years ago, I was in a long-term relationship with a remarkable woman who began as submissive to me in our relationship. Within a year she and her Eros began a shift. Her new path led her to begin training in the emerging neo-Tantric arts, and she connected with a circle of practitioners in that arena across the USA.

By then, we had such a deep, loving, spiritual connection that we stayed together despite this divergence of paths. We agreed to expand the meaning of our relationship and create a big enough container to include other submissive's on my side, and her Tantric lovers and more relevantly, clients on her side.

We often socialized with the other sacred-sex workers when we traveled or they came to our city. While all discussion was anonymous to protect confidentiality, we engaged in many discussions of what their clientele profile looked like and their client's desires. My partner and I also engaged in many talks about these subjects, often right after she emerged from one of her sessions!

It was at this stage that a new point of view emerged regarding my judgments of a married partner seeking out sex behind their partner's backs. My partner's clientele was composed primarily of married men, and in some cases women, who sought out her ritual Tantric practices.

I had numerous Tantric, or more accurately neo-Tantric oriented encounters with my partner, several of the Tantric friends in our circle, and had attended numerous workshops on sacred-sexuality practices over the 6 years we were together. I had a pretty good sense of what my partner's clients sought in their sessions with her, and what they may receive.

The essence of these ancient, sacred, sexual arts in contemporary form was a loving embrace of the masculine by the feminine, through the channel of surrender by the masculine to the "goddess" or divine feminine.

In the westernized version known as neo Tantra, these sacred sexuality sessions are held in a luscious, enlivened, ambient setting, and often begin with the client and practitioner sitting across from each other, breathing, eye-gazing, and shedding the outside reality to begin entering into an altered reality, steeped in sacred Eros.

Ambiance is employed in the form of scent, color, sound and texture throughout the ritual space, further soothing the client's body, mind and soul, to allow the feminine to be beheld, admired and worshipped. This would then move on to conscious touch by hands, then body to body embrace led by the feminine, while the masculine simply but deeply received, breathed and let Erotic energy rise within them on its journey to bliss.

Ideally, in this ritual feminine embodiment, there was no threat, judgment, manipulation, humiliation or diminishment of the masculine. The client was being embraced, adored, cherished, beheld and forgiven both physically and spiritually. Some men could be brought to tears, overwhelmed by a sense of welcome they had never received from the feminine. And while breathing the energy of their sexual arousal, sans story, fantasy or attachment, up from their root chakra to their crown, the man could be brought to a convulsive ecstatic release at the skilled coaching of the Tantrika's hands. In the trade the service is known as a "Holy Hand-job!"

Previous to this experience with my partner and our Tantric friends, I had held a firm boundary around working as a professional Dom with married clients without their partner's clear consent. But my deeper understanding of the client's view brought me to understand the issue was far more complex than vows of honesty and fidelity with a committed partner, as important as those vows are.

Many of these clients were held to one-sided, unspoken agreements within the relationship, as far as sex goes. These silent agreements about sex were most often skewed to one partner's side...the side that was more fearful of sex, judgmental of sex, inexperienced about sex, mismatched to their partner's erotic mythos, or traumatized sexually, either physically or emotionally at some earlier point in their life. One partner in the relationship could completely control when and if sex would occur. Sex in such a relationship could have become sparse if accomplished at all. The decision to have sex, or even intimate, romantic touching, was in the hands of the less inclined partner.

Many of my former partner's male client's fit the profile of a man who had been married 20-30 years, had not had affairs, and generally loved and chose to remain with their partner, despite no place for their erotic or sensual drives to be a part of their life.

Was it really spelled out clearly in the marriage or partner agreement that one partner would control all sexual relations, even if that meant none. Was the other partner explicitly, and with full disclosure, agreeing to live for the rest of their life with a partner who was basically anti-sex, anti-affection, or who shared none of their partner's sexual desires?

I would say the answer is an emphatic no! At least for someone with an enlivened and active, if not hidden sexuality.

So I considered these and other factors that would come into play, in whether it was justified to offer my guidance services to someone married, who chose not to inform their partner. I considered how much stress the sex-deprived partner was placed under physically, emotionally and spiritually. How did this stress show up in the relationship? Was the sex-deprived partner driven to meekness, indifference, ambivalence, and unable or afraid to stand up or speak out about the sexual aspects of the relationship? Was there a state of mounting conflict or irritability and tension created between the partners? Did the deprived partner take their sexuality into secretive expressions that in some ways demeaned or added further shame, or even posed danger to the partners and the relationship? Was the repressed sex-drive rerouted to other dysfunctional behaviors, or were these stored and volatile erotic tensions even attacking the client's body, affecting health and well-being?

Would a suffering relationship suffer more, or less, if one partner discretely found a welcoming, compassionate, non-judgmental skilled sexual guide to release the accumulated tension of forced abstinence? Would the opportunity to be with a skilled compassionate sex-worker allow them to feel honored for their sexual desires; encouraged to share their fears and concerns; confess their guilt and shame; feel more safe, vulnerable and open? Would exploring with a sex-worker be a detriment to the relationship or not? Could the experience of the body becoming enlivened, their soul and passion stirred to fullness, embracing all of who they were in the present moment, all that they deserved to feel, be an explicit disregard for their love for their partner?

Based on self-reported client feedback within the neo Tantric community, these clandestine excursions into Eros, despite the clear risks, were on the whole positive. The client's expressed that the sessions provided a place for them to experience and express their sexuality that was otherwise lacking. Having an outlet for this expression helped reduce stress, resentment and conflict about sex within their relationship. For numerous clients the overwhelming need went beyond the sexual. They needed most to be lovingly, warmly touched and embraced by a woman, a too infrequent occurrence in their relationship. This aspect was significantly positive and important to the client.

In this era there are more and more pro Dommes adding this conscious, mindful, compassionate regard to their services as well.

I recognize that the context of what I have written to this point is only examining the lack of sex or affection in relationships as described from the male side. There is of course, their partner's side. The male client's spoken of above certainly shared the responsibility for the disconnected state of their relationship. They may have been terrible communicators, inept sexually or romantically, or brought their own unresolved baggage and trauma into the relationship, that prevented both partners from achieving the intimacy they deserved.

I also note that the previous pages were focused on men in the relationship as being the one's deprived. From my personal and professional experience working with many women clients and research data from my PEM survey, this is certainly not the case. The majority of clients for Tantric practitioners spoken of here are men and the practitioners are women. The fact is that traditionally, most of the clientele in all sex-worker categories are men. That trend is turning a bit as more and more women are acknowledging they are suffering the same fate of deprivation…and more and more women are doing something about it.

If you haven't already, I encourage you to do the same in whatever way is right for you. Claim your sexual birthright. Love and be proud of who you are sexually. Explore and experiment liberally. Untangle every internalized resistance that judges, shames or fears your empowered sexual expression. Be conscious, in integrity, transparent with your partners. Seek to create greater trust and compassion. Negotiate honestly and keep your agreements. Listen well. Practice techniques to be mindful, embodied and present. Let your Sex Creature be as wild, perverse and Kinky as it truly is. Enjoy!

If you are already on your own sexually authentic journey, bless you. You are the vanguard. You are pioneering a new advancement in human evolution. You are aligned with reintegrating the body, sensual pleasure, sexual diversity, intimacy, trust, consent, healing shame, fear and trauma, inviting honesty and for some of us, the most intense sexual pleasure imaginable! Thank you for leading the way!

ADDENDUM:

Note: *The following is an academic paper I submitted to a professional journal, so it has quotes and APA style references. It provides certain arguments and rationales, some that have been stated previously in this book, and new material as well, but also includes peer-reviewed references to broaden the argument.*

It is my hope that the therapeutic professions continue to evolve and open to accepting and understand that those who identify as Fetishsexuals should be included within the normal range of recognized sexual identities. For additional views on expanding the therapy professions approach to supporting those coming to terms with their sexuality see my lecture: **Redefining Sex Therapy for 21ˢᵗ Century Sexuality**

FETISHSEXUALITY AS AN AUTHENTIC SEXUAL IDENTITY
THE EMPOWERING AND HEALING POTENTIAL WITHIN OUR MOST TABOO DESIRES

Introduction

My intention is to convey a preliminarily researched foundation for expanding the current psychological designations of sexual identity (straight, bi, gay or lesbian) to include an identity I call Fetishsexuality. A Fetishsexual, by my definition, is a person driven to orgasm or other deep erotic state through their innate, inherent, lifelong desire for a particular range of dominance, submission, sadism, masochism, aka Kink or Fetish and other symbol-driven erotic expressions. Overall, Fetish or Kink has a much grander sweep of potential alternative sexual practices, desires, and inclinations than listed above (Fetlife, 2013).

In the larger scope, this paper will point to the value of sexual authenticity in any of its many forms, and the empowering and healing depths that may be available when anyone embraces their sexual truth in a conscious, aware manner. What constitutes approaching and exploring one's authentic sexual desire in a conscious manner will be considered as well.

Sexual authenticity, in my experience, requires a conscious effort to differentiate one's true erotic desire, and its deepest nuances within the erotic unconscious, from the embedded shame, fear, trauma, and harsh internalized judgments that may resist if not totally dominate the desire. It is through this effort to untangle erotic desire from the shame, fear, and judgment that may hold it back, that the empowering and healing potential inherent in this exploration may be found.

Authentic Sexuality Overview

Up until very recently, as far as the clinical psychological model was concerned, fetish-oriented sexuality was viewed as a pathology, or as the negatively described term for a psychological sexual disorder, a paraphilia (American Psychiatric Association, 2013). My experience and my work with hundreds of clients and workshop participants over the last 15 years, whose clear desire and intent was to come to terms with, explore, and understand their fetish-driven sexuality, leads me to conclude that the pathological model is far from the only view to describe the nature of Fetishsexuality. To the greatest extent, clients sought my help to untangle their authentic life-long fetish desires from the embedded shame, fear, and harsh judgments that resisted their desire. It was not unusual for clients in their 40s or 50s to divulge that I am the first person they had ever revealed their desire to. For decades, they had hidden their desires from their partners, spiritual guides, and traditional therapists. It did not feel safe to even talk about their desires, let alone enact them. It is the intent of my work to contribute to creating a safer therapeutic, academic, political and social environment for people to share their erotic truths without fear of being harshly judged, condemned, or ostracized.

Based on these direct experiences with clients and sex research findings, I hope to illuminate how and why Fetishsexuality is an innate aspect of one's psyche that can and should be engaged in a conscious, aware, mature, healthy manner by those so inclined. I will attempt to define and describe the various and considerable depths of personal empowerment and healing that conscious engagement of one's Fetishsexuality may offer, at least for the portion of the human gene pool that I believe are innately and authentically Fetishsexuals.

This chapter will also examine the ways that unconscious personal and collective myths, archetypes, and symbols are or may be woven into the fabric of authentic Fetishsexuality as well as the ways that threads of unconscious shame, trauma, fear, and judgment get tangled up and inhibit or thwart authentic sexual expression. Such entanglements, I believe, can lead to the problematic shadow manifestations of sexual secrecy, dishonesty, and other diminishments of one's personal integrity.

Evolution of Sexual Viewpoints

Until a few decades ago, any but the most fundamental sexual activities had been classified either by law, religion, or mental health providers as deviant, immoral, or in psychological terms, a paraphilia (DSM-V, 2013). In other words, most people engaging in fetish sexual practices were considered to be engaging in either an illegal or an immoral act, or had a psychological disorder, or all three. In more recent times, the landscape of sexual identity and the pantheon of sexual practices an adult may choose to participate in have been coming into a better and broader focus. It is my opinion that the narrow and shallow views of the previous theories of human sexuality (Berry, 2013) are not effective at holding the burgeoning reality of human sexuality that has erupted over the last 30 years, since the dawn of the Internet era. I further believe that recognizing Fetishsexuality as a sexual identity would open the way for more nuanced and effective psychological models of the sexual psyche to take shape and, hopefully, lead to new therapeutic models that better support one in embracing his or her sexual authenticity, and healing all the ways it may have been traumatized, condemned, judged, feared, hated or hidden.

Currently, only heterosexual, gay/lesbian, and bi-sexual are considered sexual orientations or identities according to the American Psychological Association (APA). From my research so far, that there is no scientifically confirmed methodology for determination of sexual identity; rather, it seems defined in subjective terms by the APA (2010).

Sexual orientation refers to an enduring pattern of emotional, romantic, and/or sexual attractions to men, women, or both sexes. Sexual orientation also refers to a person's sense of identity based on those attractions, related behaviors, and membership in a community of others who share those attractions. . . . Therefore, sexual orientation is not merely a personal characteristic within an individual. Rather, one's sexual orientation defines the group of people in which one is likely to find the satisfying and fulfilling romantic relationships that are an essential component of personal identity for many people.

Another section of the above article cites "innate and inherent, or life-long" as integral characteristics of sexual orientation. I believe it is quite evident, from my experience of working with hundreds of people and observing that millions of people are engaging with others in various fetish communities, events and activities proliferating around the world, that there exists a sizable portion of the human gene-pool that has an innate and inherent Fetishsexual Identity (Fetlife, 2013, para. 1).

The persistent constraint of human sexuality within the very narrow parameters of mainstream definitions of "normal," (Bernstein, 2009) has inhibited a considerable portion of the population from considering and accepting their sexual desires in a more profound and meaningful way. This has resulted in what I consider to be a deep sexual shadow pervasive in the culture (Moore, 1990), not only for those with a Fetishsexual Identity but from any sex-positive or sexually honest view in any regard.

I believe that this shadow has generated unconscious, repressed, vilified, shamed, demonized, secret, and conflicted views about one's personal sexuality, views that are prevalent throughout the minds of the majority of my clients as well as the culture collectively. These negatively judgmental internal messages we carry about our authentic sexual feelings, and the fear of others judgment, has led to our cultural inability to be honest about our sexual desires. The issue of our sexual dishonesty is systemic. The widespread reportage of partners having affairs behind each other's backs, secret porn usage, visiting sex providers on the sly, and other such manifestations is pandemic (Parker-Pope, 2008). This sexual dishonesty has created a culture where sex is debased and pushed down below the surface. It becomes the forbidden fruit. We do not know how to talk with our partners about our sexual desires, to be honest about them, share, explore, or revel in them. We are supposed to aspire to be sexy on one hand of the cultural messaging and yet not look at others in a sexual way or express our sexuality overtly on the other. There is an implied normalcy that we are judged by in all these regards.

What normal *is* is never defined. Normal is . . . you know . . . normal! However, there is a never-ending stream of opinion and even law about what is *not* normal. If there is not a law, there is a harsh social, religious, or familial pressure, if not outright violence, to conform to normal, also known as moral or civilized (Klein, 2008). Witness the history of the gay and lesbian movements' struggle to normalize the truth of their identities (Williams, 2003).

As I view it, our authentic sexuality is tangled up in outdated, archaic, and irrelevant moral and religious doctrines designed for a cultural mindset equivalent to the medieval Dark Ages. It is my opinion that humanity has reached a point in evolution where sexuality is busting loose from the ultimately flimsy bonds of fear-driven moralities about the flesh and the more instinctive and primal dimensions of human behavior.

This fear about sex and the fear about our partner or anyone else knowing the truth of our sexual desire on the one hand, and the astronomical, internet-driven rise in sexual interest and desire clearly emerging in the culture on the other, are on a collision course. We cannot be honest about our sexual desire, and we cannot stop our sexual desire from acting out. This may be a recipe for psycho-dramatic mayhem at all levels of American culture. The continuous stream of politicians, church leaders, and celebrities falling from grace when exposed in pursuit of their secret pleasures is just the tip of the iceberg of the enormous sexual shadow of the culture at large, in my judgment.

Core Aspects of Fetish Sexual Identity

I will now focus on what I surmise are the core components of Fetishsexuality and consider how those may operate through both conscious and unconscious aspects of the personal and collective psyche. In this regard, it is my experience that someone with a Fetishsexual identity also has what I define as a Personal Erotic Myth (PEM) that is engaged, from within the unconscious, when they become sexually aroused.

A PEM contains the fantasy imagery, storylines, mythic personas, props, attire, dialogue and actions that drive a person who has a PEM to orgasm or other deep erotic states. This mythos and the attendant archetypal persona is often expressed in Fetish, Kink, and D/s-BDSM oriented sex, where symbol, myth and archetypal personifications abound (Fetlife, 2013). Some people are quite aware of their PEM and their particular personification in the inner myth – Dominant or submissive for instance. For others, their full erotic nature is still buried in the unconscious but shows up in private reveries or brief moments within sexual engagement with a partner. Many may have caught glimpses of it, or engaged it secretly, even well before puberty. In my ongoing *Discover Your Personal Erotic Myth Survey*, over 2000 anonymous respondents drawn from a sex-positive and alternative population, nearly 60% stated

177

that they had begun having sexual fantasies before 10 years of age. Furthermore, 40% stated they were already masturbating to their fantasies by 10 years of age. Over 70% self-identified as believing that their sexuality was driven by their PEM (Fous, 2012). I speculate from this data, and anecdotally through similar reporting from client's, that one hallmark of a Fetishsexual identity may be that someone's erotic inclinations were already alive and active well before puberty. This speculation is drawn only from my preliminary research and is speculation in its broadest sense. Yet, it is quite intriguing to find a high percentage of the survey sample reporting distinct erotic desires and enactments prior to puberty.

From the millions of people participating in fetish-driven dating sites and social media (No1 Reviews, 2013), it is clear that many have already crossed the threshold from secrecy holding them back to engaging the desire itself. Some people may have multiple PEMs that ebb and flow in their sex life. For many others, it is still an unconscious but compelling force, just below acknowledged awareness, that drives their sexual desire. This is the aspect of their Eros that they may not have looked at nor engaged in consciously, however, during sex, in the last moments right before orgasm, their authentic erotic persona, or "sex creature" as I sometimes think of it, can flood into the body in wild, fierce gestures, accompanied by profane, blasphemous invectives — sound-bytes from their PEM (Fous, 2012).

Frommer (2007) alludes to these unconscious mythic dimensions of Eros and how research on the psychology of Eros is sorely lacking in more mainstream therapeutic models:

> *This otherness reflects aspects of self-experience that come forward during lustful states of mind — hidden, transgressive, dis-avowed parts of ourselves that gain expression in erotic contexts. Think, for example, of sexual fantasies and enactments that hinge on a desire for dominance, submission or surrender in which a more familiar sense of self is altered. . . . It is this highly subjective dimension of self-experience in erotic contexts — the conscious and unconscious experiences of self and*

self-other relations—that has been both neglected and under-theorized in psychoanalytic explorations of sexuality, except when the expression of one's desire is deemed problematic or perverse. (p. 34)

There are currently few to no institutions, academic or otherwise, that I am aware of, that teach, study, or look at Fetish or Kink driven sexuality as anything but an odd perversion, something to spice up one's sex life, or a deviant disorder, if not an outright pathology rather than as one's normal sexuality that is distinct from others. In my opinion, this is as large an oversight and as inane as the discounting and pathologizing of gay or lesbian sexuality had been before the recent era.

Therapists who go into couples or relationship counseling, as far as I can tell, are not required to explore their own sexual desires, to be aware of the inner judgments or projections they may place on clients, or even to have examined or resolved the ways their own sexuality may have been traumatized, denied, or repressed due to their immersion in a sex-negative culture (Salazar, 2006). Yet, they are sanctioned as the "qualified" licensed providers of sex-therapy by government, professional, academic institutions and insurance providers.

Sexologist Dennis Dailey (1988) describes his view of how the patient experience can be negatively affected by the therapist. He asserts that too many therapists have no skill or training in the nature of sexuality nor in the treatment of patients who come to them with these concerns:

Too often those who experience the need or desire for help in sex-related concerns encounter helpers who reflect the harsh, judgmental, inaccurate and narrow perspectives on sexuality which still exist in our society. . . . Too often the sexually unusual do not experience helpful encounters, but in fact are frequently harmed by the helping process. (p. 166)

I believe that it is critically important to support all constructive efforts to introduce what might be generally called sex-positive therapy models into mainstream academic curricula and the helping professions, ones that expand on the inroads already underway in gay and lesbian sexual theory. I am aware of one independent professional psychological organization that generally takes this sex-positive approach, the American Association of Sex Educators, Counselors and Therapists (AASECT).

Recent research in evolutionary theory around sexuality also seems to support viewing alternative sexual desires in a new light, beyond typical psychological, religious, or moral perspectives (Gardner, 1993):

> The many different types of human sexual behavior, including the paraphilias, can be seen as having species survival value. These atypical sexual behaviors all, in some way enhance the general level of sexual excitation in society and therefore increase the likelihood that people will engage in sexual activities that lead to procreation. (p. 47).

Human Sexuality, it seems, is still a great and vast wilderness area of human psychology. We hardly allow ourselves to look at it, except in sneaky or shy glances. This keeps the territory of Eros dark, obscure, and out of view, which is certainly proper in its way, but it is also concealing, giving cover to the destructive shadows of our sexual expression (Moore, 1990). Because of people's fear or not knowing how to be honest about their desires with their partners, they often choose instead to sneak, hide, repress, deny, project, or engage in other harmful behaviors that damage their well-being, and ultimately, their relationships. This has been the state of humans' relationship to sexuality for millennia. It seems absolutely dysfunctional to me that something obviously as huge a part of who we are as our sexuality does not see the light of day, does not get put under the microscope, does not get studied with the same serious scrutiny, wonder, and fervor to understand as every other aspect of the human experience of life on earth is studied. I am personally excited to feel engaged at the frontier of a new era of sexual awareness, honesty, study, and expansion into the deeper uncharted realms of Eros. As Berry (2013) frames it,

...in essence, many sex therapists may equate the psychosexual dimension of psychoanalysis with Oedipal theory, or classical theories of neurosis. To learn that contemporary psychoanalysis can offer sophisticated clinical insights on a range of sexual phenomena—including the nature of unconscious fantasy and intimacy, sexuality and gender, sexual aggression, unconscious hostility, and the meaning of penetration— might significantly change many sex therapists' perspective on the usefulness of psychoanalysis. (p. 13)

Unpacking the Myth

What is a Personal Erotic Mythos? For many, this concept may be foreign. In a repressed culture that greatly denies or frowns on the pleasures of the body and sexual fantasy, most have not ventured very far in understanding the unconscious sexual story lines that may be playing out during sexual engagement, or even more so, in solitary masturbatory revelry (Fous, 2012). I know from my own experience when I was younger and from working with clients the last 15 years that the truth of these inner erotic stories or myths were often only glimpsed briefly, right before the frenzied liberation of orgasm. In that last minute or so before orgasm, the truth of one's Eros, or as I define it, one's PEM, can no longer be hidden and bursts wildly forth into the body and through the suddenly unconstrained voice in a truncated blasphemy, such as "Oh, God, fuck me. YES! Harder, take it, deeper, shit, slut, whore, fucker, bitch," and less decipherable, primitive grunts and screams. These are just sound-bytes as I consider it, from one's full PEM, for those with a Fetishsexual identity.

In the typical lights-out sex most of us have experienced, these last moments before orgasm can reveal, in furious sounds and frenzied physical abandonment, snippets from what is like a highly-compacted zip file of one's Erotic myth. In this context, it is being played out in the subconscious mind and experienced in the crescendo of orgasm, similar to the super speedy talk of the guy

181

reading the disclaimers at the end of those pharmaceutical commercials or car sale ads. Only way faster!

If people with a PEM that was still held primarily in the unconscious were able to slow that moment of orgasm way down and observe what is really going on, they could begin to uncover, I believe, the myth that drives them to orgasm. Within that packed and condensed zip file, there is a rich, compelling story. It is a story generated and played out deep within the unconscious Erotic psyche when someone engages in sex, at least someone with a Fetishsexual identity, driven by a Personal Erotic Myth. Like any story, there is a prologue, setting, props, attire, counterparts, dialogue, body language, and action (Fous, 2013). Additionally, there are mythic archetypal personas taking part in the story, each representing a dyad drawn from a pantheon of pairs in the collective Erotic archives of the human psyche. Some classic archetypal pairs commonly found in personal ads on fetish dating sites are Daddy/Daughter, Mistress or Master/Slave, Bad Boy/Good Girl, Supreme Bitch/Cuckold, and many more (Fetlife, 2013). There are hundreds of variations. Someone may have a single major theme or may shift into a variety of these pairings, and some even reverse which side they take. There also can be an over-riding sense of Dominance and Submission at play and all manner of what may be, for the explorer, intoxicatingly perverse immersions into myths that carry a very potent and ecstatic erotic charge.

In my research so far and from my work with clients, I feel there could be aspects of these mythic erotic stories rooted in or connected to embedded psychological constructs from more primitive levels of evolution, consciousness, and behaviors (Gardner, 1993). Although I hope to do more research about the instinctual, primitive aspects of our sexuality in the future, I will make a few unverified notations here. These instinctual manifestations may be rooted, I believe, in the unconscious psychological structures that are part of our heritage biologically and psychologically, from our reptilian (predator/prey archetypes) and mammalian (Alpha/beta pecking orders) heritage. These aspects of our humanity have been shoved below the surface through the "civilizing" we have undergone as a species over the last several thousand years. Being civilized, cultivated, rational, refined, and sophisticated is the mask humans strive to maintain over our more primitive, instinctual, wild natures. However, humans are far from civilized, in my view, and the beast within runs rampant across the world, savaging individuals, families, communities, cultures, countries, and the environment, as has been the state of the civilized world since civilization began (Moore, 1990). The cold-blooded, predatory reptile and the blood-thirsty, domineering, territorial mammal are aspects of human nature that show up nightly in the evening news' broadcasts of the rampant abuse of power, barbarism, and brutality that individuals or groups might deploy on their family, friends, strangers, and foes. Interestingly, these behaviors are also similar and, in many regards, common to the archetypal themes and personifications in many of the hundreds of PEMs I have reviewed of people venturing into the realms of Kink and Fetishsexuality. These themes can occur consensually on both sides of the power equation in these potent ritual erotic exchanges Fetishsexuals participate in.

From my experience and by the self-evident opt-in of millions of people on fetish porn dating and other sites, some significant portion of the population has an inherent fetish-driven sexual nature, held within a PEM(s), just as around 5% to 10% of the gene pool is estimated to be gay or lesbian in their sexual orientation (Crary, 2011). I speculate that Fetishsexuality may be a much higher percentage. I would assert that Fetishsexuality is a valid sexual orientation, similar to gay or lesbian orientation. It is innate, inherent, and does not go away. It is one's sexual orientation for life. It cannot be disowned. It does not need to be fixed or extracted, though many push it down into shadow where it may leak out in disturbing, risky, dangerous, or compulsive behaviors.

One of the more enlightened approaches I have found to help people embrace their sexual truths and capacities, and deal with ways they may be unhealthy or withheld, comes from the work of Jack Morin (1995). Morin developed a model of sexual expression based on what he called a Core Erotic Theme (CET), which comes very close to the concept of a PEM. However, whereas a PEM is inherent and not shaped from the environment; a CET, in Morin's view, represents sexuality shaped by some earlier experience of neglect or trauma. One's alternative sexual inclinations are unconscious efforts to fulfill or compensate for what was lacking as a child rather than the pursuit of their inherent authentic Eros. According to Morin,

> *...at the most fundamental level, your CET is an amazingly efficient shorthand encapsulating crucial situations about which people, situations and images tend to evoke your most forceful genital and psychic responses. The CET however, is far more than a mere checklist of what and who turns you on. Its extraordinary power arises from the fact that it links today's compelling turn-ons with crucial challenges and turmoils from the past. Hidden within your CET is a formula for transforming unfinished emotional business from childhood and adolescence into excitation and pleasure.* (p. 141)

While this CET phenomenon could certainly be the case to some degree, for anyone who is engaged in an unconscious expression of their sexuality, these "unfinished" aspects that may be tangled up from the past with one's authentic sexual truth would be differentiated and treated independently for someone wishing to embrace their Fetishsexual identity on its own terms. Morin's view still treats Fetishsexuality as pathology, something shaped by one's childhood experience, that is now being compensated for through one's alternative sexual expression, rather than as one's normal innate sexuality.

It is still a challenge at all levels of society, I believe, to hold those with a Fetishsexual identity in a healthy, respectful regard, without the constant judgment that these "poor souls" must have been damaged or traumatized in some way. What seems damaging and traumatic, to me, are the outdated cultural, moral, social, political, legal, therapeutic and religious codes that tend or are intended to make people feel afraid, ashamed, immoral, criminal, pathological, sick, disgusting, or dangerous regarding their authentic sexuality (Stein, 2008). Fetishsexuals are, in my opinion, about a generation behind the gay and lesbian communities in being recognized as valid representations of human sexual diversity.

In actuality, the traumas, shaming's, and harsh internalized moral judgments inflicted on many people with a Fetishsexual identity as they grew up, have gotten tangled up with their natural sexual desires. This situation has left many people frozen and unable to express their innate desires joyfully without simultaneously feeling guilty, ashamed, or afraid of their own desires and can leave them feeling stuck psychologically, emotionally, and sexually, or shut down or disconnected.

Anatomy of a Personal Erotic Myth

I will present here some aspects of how I work with clients in support of their intention to embrace their sexual authenticity, discover, express and illuminate their PEM, and then discover and untangle the unconscious parts of their psyche that resist or object to their erotic desires. Following are notes from a recent case study with a female client (Fous, 2013), over the course of 3 sessions. Her process highlights the challenges and efforts people may face to integrate their authentic sexual nature into their everyday life, and in this case, within an already established long-term partnership.

My client fits, with some precision, into my concept of someone whose sexual path to orgasm or other deep erotic state, is driven by a PEM. Her PEM formed decades ago, and, as is the case for many with a Fetishsexual identity, she was sexually aware and engaged before she had reached puberty (Gardner, 1993). In my experience working with hundreds of people over the past 15 years, fetish desires are rarely connected to pathologies generated from early age traumas or other environmental factors, as many are led to believe

(Morin, 1995). In my view, a fetish-driven sexuality is as innate and inherent as is being gay or lesbian.

My client was a woman in her mid-40s, with a particular lifelong desire for rough sex, Daddy/Daughter play, dressing slutty, and other taboo yearnings that she had been unable to share with past partners. She was currently in an eight-year relationship with a man who was very sweet and loving but was not the aggressive masculine persona who inhabited her desires. She had reached a place where she knew her desire was demanding to be expressed, even to the point of leaving her relationship if necessary, when she sought me out for support. Her work with me offers a comprehensive over-view of many of the complexities of expressing one's authentic de-sire and encountering the shadows/wounds/fears/shames/judg-ments that are inevitably part of the process.

I believe that the overview offered here maps out well the inner terrain and operation of this client's Personal Erotic Myth. Her case also models the opportunities as well as the complex resistances that can be encountered in bringing these desires into one's personal awareness and experience, and then into one's relationships, in a conscious manner. With her partner's permission and support, my client chose to explore the fetish aspects of her sexuality, on her own, with hopes of then bridging this desire to include her partner at some future time.

One aspect of this client's challenge to integrate her Fetish-sexuality into her life in a conscious way was rooted in her relation-ship to her partner. She described how her partner had been strug-gling with feeling that he is not the kind of man that could be what she seemed to be seeking. He felt threatened by her attraction to the strong, forceful masculine, and she feared he would get triggered into own his pain/wounding of not being good enough if she ex-pressed her desire for a more forceful masculinity during sex. She described her partner's conflict "between being raised by his mother to believe fighting is for animals, that a good man is a gentle man," and her desire for him to take her forcefully. Here we have an illus-

186

tration of how paradox comes into play. My client was seeking an aggressive masculinity, even a transgressive masculinity in her mythic fantasies. She did not seek to be violated in their day-to-day relationship. Her partner, at this point, was unable to embrace the paradox that he could be the gentle, good man he aspired to be in everyday life and in a negotiated engagement with his partner, also be aggressive, rough, and selfish in the realms of Eros. Although it did not turn out to be the case here, this level of examination of one's sexual authenticity is also the place where an erotic mismatch might be uncovered in a relationship. In my experience, this is not an uncommon occurrence when couples have not included a clear, negotiated, detailed discussion around the sexual mythos of each partner before beginning the relationship.

My client described how she was an early sexual explorer, masturbating by age 5, engaging other little girls to play with her, and continuing her exploration well into puberty. She had gotten caught a couple of times, once at home by her parents, once with a girlfriend. When the friend's parents discovered her play with their daughter, around age 10, the parents scolded her for her shameful behavior and forbade her from seeing their daughter again. Through this and other episodes and an overall sense of shame around her active sexuality, the client had generally been unable to verbalize or share her fantasies with her adult lovers. For a long time, she felt sure that something was wrong with her, "that [she] would have to envision being raped or punished against [her] will in order to have an orgasm." In the first session, I worked with this client to support her in differentiating the part of her that held the fetish desires from the part of her that held those desires in shame and judgment. This included some forms of conscious movement, discussion, and imaginal processes to help bring her desire to a more conscious and visible view, and begin to untangle it from what kept it repressed.

The first session was so powerful. I finally met this young girl who has been with me, in my fantasies or mythic desire, as you call it, in nearly every orgasm throughout my life. . . . I felt so enlivened, so awakened by the experience. I met this wanton young girl who could not own her own wild desire and so incurred the wrath/or desire of those in authority (father, teacher, priest, doctor) to control her, punish her, deliver to her exactly what she wanted. (Fous, 2013)

In our subsequent sessions, through further conscious movement and embodiment processes, we worked further on releasing shame and the fear of judgment her desire had been encased in physically. Additionally, we created and employed ritual physical enactments that allowed dimensions of her erotic persona to be embodied and expressed, and then discussed strategies of how to bring her discoveries and deeper sense of who she was back into her relationship. By the third session, she was ready to move forward and engage with her partner.

This exploration into my shadow, my secret fantasies, my submerged sexual identities, began as a solo journey. I wanted to taste the experience of what was in my head when I orgasm without having to process or consider my current partner's feelings and fears. When I brought him into my explorations, I was surprised and relieved to hear that he would like to know this young girl in my inner myth that he wants to love all of me. I knew from the many times he's told me, that he could see her often when we make love. I was encouraged to reveal my fantasies with him as I'd never done with any man before. . . . I see new excitement in my lover, and I'm relieved and excited myself to begin to more intentionally and consciously explore this realm with my man. (Fous, 2013)

Differentiating Desire From Resistance

The "work" I do with a client in this dimension of the erotic wilderness is edgy by most standards and branches into uncharted territory as far as client/therapist interactions go. What it looks like will vary according to the individual circumstances of the client. The main components are an initial discussion to determine the scope of the client's desire, what conflicts with the desire, the client's relevant history, and what the client wants as an outcome of our work together.

From here, the work can be simply to discuss, question, and develop an ongoing, practical, clear strategy for negotiating what one wants in the real world. Deeper inquiries may begin to uncover and separate out or differentiate specific aspects of the desire and the conflicted or resistant parts that are tangled up unconsciously with the desire. These entanglements often negatively affect or thwart the client's intention to be who they are sexually. This initial inquiry would be used to first illuminate one's current relation to past sexual trauma, if that is part of the client's history, and to understand how that is impacting one's intention to come to terms with the desire. These deeper inquiries would also support the client to self-assess inner judgments, shames, and fears expressed in unconscious messages about their authentic sexuality and sexuality in general, that the client took on from family, religion, and culture. These internalized messages can often have power over one's desire and the intention to express it. There might be processes and practices co-developed to help illuminate and empower the desire and resolve, heal, and diminish the power held by the inner judgments, fears, or shames. There might be other imaginal processes involved to help clients access unconscious material to "flesh out" and bring to precise conscious awareness the who/what/where of their desires. The path is intended to lead clients to the place of empowerment where they have fully differentiated, honored, welcomed, and embraced their authentic sexual mythos. At the same time, they can begin to heal and disengage any mythos of shame, fear, or judgment about their sexuality from their emotional and physical landscape and, finally, develop a healthy, mature strategy to begin to integrate their newly normative Eros into their everyday life. I often encourage clients to develop a regular personal ritual practice to stay connected to and deepen their intention and further resolve shame, fear, judgments or other that may need ongoing support.

Some psychological theories of what shapes normative and non-normative sexuality follow a model that one's inherent sexual identity is warped and shaped by the repressive, sex-negative culture it is immersed in or the way it has been terrorized. In speaking of the formation of sexuality in gay men, Frommer (2007) writes:

> To the extent that generic statements can be made about desire, the meaningful distinction to be drawn between non-normative and normative desire is between desire that is marked by stigma, i.e., spoiled identity (Goffman, 1963) and desire that is not. When erotic desire violates social imperatives, the emergence of that desire within the psyche is shaped by and through that stigmatization. In a homophobic and heterosexist culture, experiences involving shame and narcissistic vulnerability are ubiquitous in the lives of men who offend gender through their expression of same-sex desire. Shame, as I am conceiving it, does not merely compromise or inhibit desire; it becomes part of the weave of desire itself, actually shaping it. (p. 37)

It is my view that what Frommer describes represents desire entangled with shame, which will certainly impact how desire will or can be expressed. However, his identification of this situation seemingly stops there. That is the way it is! My belief and experience is that it is possible and imperative to untangle the embedded cultural or religious mythos of shame in the unconscious from the authentic erotic mythos of the individual. They are two separate and distinct personas. The shame mythos taints, interferes with, or fully prohibits the physical, emotional, and psychological expression of the authentic erotic desire. There is also the potential that someone's PEM involves their being ritually shamed or degraded in a way that has a compelling and desirable erotic charge, but in no way reflects any actual traumatic experience they had growing up. In this case, an erotic encounter done within a safe, conscious, negotiated ritual with a trusted partner is exactly what should be condoned in support of authentic sexual expression.

In the case where a client's authentic sexuality is tangled in shame, in my experience, there is often a strong body correlation. Their authentic sexual expression, emotionally and physically, and their liveliness in general is encumbered by the weights and chains of shame. Work at the body level will often be indicated to support the client in getting present, embodied, grounded, and prepared for whatever other work may follow. Body-centered work can also locate where these tensions are stored and begin to release the many fears, shames, and other tensions that have accumulated in the body after decades of hiding, judging, or holding back the desire (Bowen, 2011; Lowen, 1975). At an even deeper layer of the work that might open up with a client, and as was the case with the client described previously, a negotiated ritual process might be agreed on, where the therapist embodies a mythic counterpart to the persona in the myth that drives the client's desire.

As mentioned earlier, a PEM most always includes paired personas, such as Master/slave, Mommy/son, FemDom/cuckold, Daddy/daughter, Teacher/student, and a pantheon of other variations (Fous, 2012). The PEM generally includes action, dialogue, tone of voice, body language, props, attire and context. However, a PEM is not acting out a part; it is not just role-playing. It is literally embodying this alter erotic persona that one authentic-ally possesses and allowing it the unencumbered space to enter the body and express fully, without shame, guilt, or judgment. These archetypal personas operating within people's PEM are already intact and whole within the individual's personal unconscious and also reference the collective unconscious. These personas do not need to be scripted out, they just need to be allowed to embody and be present. They already know what they desire to do, say, with whom, what implements, attire, setting, and other elements common to their mythic story. The methodology has a similarity I would say to method acting, where the actor immerses in and becomes the part, while remaining who they are overall. The emphasis again is on developing conscious, consensual, negotiated risk-aware practices to allow these erotic embodiments to occur. Like Homosexuality, Fetish-sexuality does not develop as a result of a trauma induced pathology. BDSM, Kink and Fetish sexual engagements are simply what is normal for Fetishsexuals.

Based on my review of current research, it appears that my theory of the foundations of Fetish desires, the existence of a Fetish-sexual Identity, and the nature of a Personal Erotic Myth are outside the realm of current psychological theory. In terms of a therapeutic practice, my theories and practices are well beyond conventional views of what is acceptable. But I believe that this therapeutic work of empowering desire and untangling all that resists it needs to delve into these deeper nuances within the erotic psyche. It will also often need to be hands-on and interactive, in order to help clients un-cover, embrace heal, embody, experience and untangle their authen-tic desires, from the decades of denial, fear, shame, and hiding that their desire may have been pushed under.

I was pleased to find, in my research, other examples of pushing the edge of what has been a more traditional and conservative view of client-therapist relations. One example was Phelan's (2009) description of a therapy referred to as body-centered psychotherapy being used to help a client get in deeper touch with her "feelings" of being attracted or not to someone. The therapy involves a direct engagement of the client's body by the therapist in order to liberate the client's intention from the unconscious blockage that was also mirrored in the client's body.

As we began to work, Elizabeth said, "I don't know what to do. I don't know what to do with my body. I can't tell if I'm attracted to someone. I just don't know how people know these things. It's like everybody knows something that I don't know, like I was looking the wrong way one day when they taught it in school." "I don't know what to do with my body" became the central refrain in our work. Recognizing that we had entered the domain in which her previous therapy had become frozen, we decided to explore more directly her experience of her body's not knowing what to do with itself.

With this decision, Elizabeth and I moved into the domain of therapeutic activity that is unique to body-centered psychotherapy. The movement of the client's body, of the therapist's body, and movement between client and therapist become a central feature of the therapeutic endeavor. Body psychotherapy brings to conventional psychotherapy an informed and skilled attention to the activity, motility, sensorimotoric coherence, and bodily competence of the client. (p. 97)

In my own practice, working at the body level is often the first order of business in helping clients come in contact with their sexual authenticity. Many of my clients simply have never learned or even understood how to be aware of their body, how it holds fear, shame, and other feelings that have gotten stuck or accumulated. I will refer here to the chapter, "The Body as Analog of the Unconscious" (Fous, 2011), for more information on how I work with a client at the body level.

It can be incredibly complex maneuvering through the terrains of paradox that are often part of the journey into sexual authenticity. For example, one might wonder, "How can I yearn to be so perverse, taboo, and primitive in my sexual desires and also still be a good parent, partner, or social, political, or religious community member? Can I be both sacred and profane without compromising my personal integrity, agreements, and physical, emotional, mental, and spiritual well-being?" It is the essence of my work to model how an individual can consciously, safely express all of who they are in an honorable way, and to demonstrate how paradox is the natural state, the truth of who we are as humans: both sacred and profane, primitive and civilized, soulful and spiritual, and all other such polarities.

It is my experience that we live in a culture that views life in an either-or context. This view separates behavior and identity into good or evil, virtuous or sinful, primitive or civilized, and black or white. Over time in our Western monotheistic culture the so-called rational, civilized aspiration was deemed superior to the primitive, instinctual desire, and the spirit deemed superior to the flesh (Paglia, 1990). This definition placed the pleasures of the flesh, carnal yearnings, and sexual expression outside of procreation, in the same despicable depths as things only dirty, stupid, uncivilized, inferior animals would want to do and/or as a damnable sin punishable by hell or inquisitional torture. In many instances, moral, religious law shaped civil law and imprisonment or even death were a potential outcome for those who slipped into their more instinctual natures (Perez, 2005). In my opinion, this either-or context ultimately caused a severe split in the psyche and extensive confusion about what to do with the obvious abundance of carnal desire humans are prone to. Western moral and religious culture has sought to banish our wild animal heritage, our sensual bodies, our fierce passions, with impossible to uphold expectations. Ultimately, for many, Freud's (1923/2007) theories about the id, banished a considerable chunk of human sexuality into the shadowy, unconscious underworld, while trying to hold up the social mask of propriety (Berry, 2013).

Additionally, for proper genital sexual integration, the sensual and affectionate currents in the unconscious had to be functionally integrated (Freud, 1912/1961d). Dissonance between these two elements, apparent in some men's psychosexuality, was the basis of Freud's widely-quoted assertion on psychogenically impotent men: "where they love they do not desire and where they desire they cannot love" (Freud, 1912/1961d, p. 183). This theory captures the essence of Freud's Virgin-Whore dichotomy: a man had to reconcile the archetypal, virginal figure of the mother with the sexually enticing archetype of the "whore" in order to be sexually integrated and genitally functional with his wife. (p. 62)

Freud perfectly describes the either-or context in the Virgin/Whore paradox. In my opinion, the Western psyche has been generally shaped to demand of itself an aspiration to the Virgin (civilized, superior, godly) and obliteration of the Whore (primitive, inferior, satanic) (Paglia, 1990). I believe this has led to the disastrous state of sexual shadow and dishonesty that abounds in modern culture.

My theoretical model allows for both sides of the paradox to be honored, welcomed, negotiated, and expressed in ways that are conscious, reasonable, and in accord and integrity with the individual's personal values and partner agreements. This model supports clients to embrace and integrate their full authentic sexual truth. It offers full respect, admiration, and encouragement for others, while honoring all of oneself as a person who aspires to integrity, honesty, and nobility, to be a good citizen, social participant, parent, and partner.

Sexual fantasies for those with a PEM are often quite profane and taboo (Fous, 2012). They cross every barrier of impropriety and inappropriateness. They are the unconscious dark erotic realm of the shadow. They mirror and evoke the brutality, transgression, and violence running amuck in the outer world on the global, local, and personal levels, and greatly repressed within the individual. There are savage, predatory, tyrannical yearnings and their counterparts embedded deep in the erotic psyche in many PEM's. In my experience, these are not pathologies and, in fact, can be gateways to very deep yearnings and authentic expressions of the personal soul. It is hard for many to grasp that there can be anything healthy, powerful, meaningful, safe, or sane involved in integrating and embracing these desires, so innate and compelling in someone with a Fetish-sexual identity—and regard them as if they were NORMAL! (Neu, 2002):

Desires are criticizable, and the presence of fantasies may be a signal of a need for a therapy of desire. Though here one should be careful to distinguish between desires, say homosexual desires that would do no harm even if expressed, so long as they were expressed in a consensual context, and desires which would indeed do harm, and could perhaps be expressed only in a nonconsensual context. A person who can be sexually stimulated only by images of rape, or images of sex with four-year-olds, may need help to understand the source and nature of their wishes and to control any associated desires. What may be truly difficult is distinguishing between fantasies which serve as harmless safety valves and fantasies which should be taken as symptoms, as warning signs. (p. 162)

What is missing in Neu's analysis is the possibility that there may be people who are compelled by images, from both points of view (dominance and submission), of rape, underage sex, Mommy/Son and many other variations, and can engage those desires in a safe and consensual way. Any such expression of sexual fantasy seems to get instantly and solely classified as a pathological potential, in many contemporary therapeutic views (DSM, 2013). It is quite important in this era that consensual engagement of erotic desire by adults is seen as distinct from any nonconsensual violation of another person. I wish to make clear the absolute distinction between the two cases. It is interesting that Neu uses a homosexual fantasy as one that could be enacted safely. It has been only 40 years since the DSM delisted homosexuality as a pathology. Perhaps now that sadism/masochism and non-disruptive paraphilia have been delisted from the DSM (DSM-V, 2013), we are just a few decades from Fetishsexuality being included as safe in such statements and cautions as Neu puts forth. People with a consciously embraced Fetishsexual identity, by definition, have absolutely no desire to engage in their mythic sexuality in any way that is harmful to or violates another person in real world interactions. Their yearning is for the ritual embodiment of their desire in a consensual, clearly negotiated way with another mature adult.

To explore the depths of our darkest desires is a challenging but empowering and healing process. It is my premise that if these very compelling parts of us are kept in hidden and secretive shadow, they will leak out in destructive ways in other parts of our lives. I believe that we are in an unprecedented era where the soul of human Eros, after millennia of repression, is forcing humanity's hand in a way. It is time to fess up, stop pretending we have no wild or dark side, or else the havoc of the sexual shadow (repression, cheating, hiding, compulsive porning, sexual violence, or other unhealthy diversions) running amuck in the world right now will get worse.

I hope that the inclusion of a female client for my case study has been instructive in that women are as a much a part of Fetishsexuality as are men. According to my theory, Fetishsexuality is already embedded in the gene-pool in a pantheon of paired personas. This is why so many millions of Fetishsexuals, men and women both, in the current era, are actually finding a match for their desires as obscure or taboo as those desires may be (Fetlife, 2013). Even the most taboo fantasies, such as rape, are not uncommon for women and do not unequivocally imply or indicate a pathology. As one study on the correlations of rape and fantasy (Zurbriggen, 2004) points out,

> ...[one] problem with the literature on force in fantasies is that it has tended to focus only on men and only on fantasies of dominance. Yet fantasies of submission are common among women. Pelletier and Herold (1984) found that 51% of their female sample reported fantasies of being forced to submit sexually, and Knafo and Jaffe (1984) noted that the fantasy reported most frequently during intercourse for women was "I imagine that I am being overpowered or forced to surrender." This fusion of submission and sex does not, however, appear to carry the same risks as does a fusion of dominance and sex. Women who report fantasies of submission have more positive attitudes about sex (Strassberg & Lockerd, 1998) and are less sexually guilty and more open to a variety of sexual experiences (Pelletier & Herold, 1988; Strassberg & Lockerd, 1998). Moreover, although sexual fantasies of submission may be more common among survivors of childhood sexual abuse (Gold, 1991), sexual victimization as an adult is apparently not predictive of fantasies of submission (Gold, Balzano, & Stamcy, 1991). Submissive fantasies in women may therefore be one aspect of a relatively open, positive, guilt-free sexuality. (p. 41)

Future Applications of Fetishsexuality Research

The research that I am beginning into the nature of Fetishsexuality has bearing on a number of integral aspects of modern life.

One area of relevance is in regard to updating the outdated dating protocols still operating in the culture at large through the expansion of tools and protocols that invite sexual honesty. People are currently partnering and marrying, in my experience, without ever having discussed, let alone known, what each other's sexual desires look like or how frequently or what kinds of sexual expression is central to their erotic nature. This omission can lead to relationships and marriages that contain devastating erotic mismatches, which, in turn, may lead to all sorts of shadowy, hidden, dangerous, or deceptive behaviors occurring behind partners' backs or showing up in other ways that can disrupt if not destroy the relationship. I believe that people need to understand that their sexuality is innate and inherent and is it their right to include that in what they seek and offer in partnership. In my view, people knowing their PEM and the tools of how to communicate that honorably with a potential partner may be more apt to have a strong bond in their overall relationship as well as a fulfilled and well-expressed sexuality. The encouragement of sexual honesty, in my experience, and the trust in each partner it implies, offers one of the most profound potentials for intimacy couples might experience.

I believe there also could be applications from this research track that could reduce the incidence of rape, child-molestation, and other nonconsensual sexual violations. I believe the offender lives in an isolate reality of secret desire that festers and grows in the dark hidden world they hold internally. At some point in their development their taboo desires first comes alive in them. I speculate there may be a substantial "intervention" window of time between this initial activation point and when they may actually cross the threshold of violating another and the devastating repercussions of doing so.

Currently there is nothing I am aware of available in the therapeutic or preventative landscape to take advantage of this period when an intervention might still occur. I envision an inverse rape crisis line that someone yet to cross the threshold of real time violation would know they could safely and anonymously call and talk to a counselor trained to help them understand a broader perspective of their desire and avoid the horrible devastation that violating another may lead to. The intention would be to help callers understand how prevalent these desires are in the population, not be judged, threatened, or condemned, and to inform them of the potential to engage in their desire with a willing partner in a consensual, ritual way that fulfilled the desire and did no harm to themselves or others. From here they could receive a referral to a therapist specializing in Fetishsexuality. I do not assert that all violators would be responsive to this approach, but feel confident that it could apply to some significant portion of offenders, enough of a percentage to make at least further consideration of this theory worthwhile.

My hope is that others will pick up on this thread to provide a stronger research foundation and analysis on the nature and scope of Fetishsexuality.

References

American Psychology Association. (2010). *Sexual orientation and homosexuality*, n.d, para.1, retrieved from http://www.apa.org/helpcenter/sexual-orientation.aspx

American Psychiatric Association. (2013). *Diagnostic and statistical manual of mental disorders* (5th ed.). Washington, DC: Author.

Bernstein, R. (2009). *The East, the West and sex: A history of erotic encounters* . New York, NY: Alfred A. Knopf.

Berry, M. D. (2013). The History and evolution of sex therapy and its relationship to psychoanalysis. *International Journal of Applied Psychoanalytic Studies,* 10: 53–74. doi: 10.1002/aps.1315

Bookish (2103). *What is tantra? Books behind the ancient sex practice.* Retrieved from http://www.bookish.com/articles/what-is-tantra-books-detail-the-ancient-sex-practice

Bowen, B. (2011). *Psycho-physical therapy*, para. 3. Retrieved from http://www.psychophysicaltherapy.com/ppt/whythebody.html

Crary, D. (2011). Gay population in U. S. estimated at 4 million. Retrieved from http://www.huffingtonpost.com/2011/04/07/gay-population-us-estimate_n_846348.html

Dailey, D. (1988). *The sexually unusual: Guide to understanding and helping.* Binghamton, New York, NY: Haworth Press.

Fetlife (2013). *Bondage, BDSM and fetish community.* Retrieved May 29, 2013, from http://fetlife.com

Fous, G. (2011). *The body mirrors the soul.* Retrieved from http://www.galenfous.com/body-mirrors-soul/

Fous, G. (2012). *Personal erotic myth survey.* Retrieved from http://obsurvey.com/r.aspx?id=6D21827B-A66B-457B-89E3-D65E7B98765E

Fous, G. (2013). *Anatomy of a personal erotic myth—case study.* Retrieved from http://www.galenfous.com/anatomy-of-a-pem/

Freud, S. (1923/2007). *The ego and the id.* Cheshire, UK: Stellar Books.

Frommer, M. S. (2007). Desire, the social unconscious, and shame. *Psychoanalysis, Culture & Society, 12*(1), 32-37. doi:10.1057/2100106

Gardner, R. (1993). *A theory about the variety of human sexual behavior.* Retrieved from http://www.ipt-forensics.com/journal/volume5/j5_2_8.htm

Harvey, T., Harvey, D. (2013). *Tantra and relationship tips.* Retrieved from http://www.huffingtonpost.com/thea-and-duane-harvey/relationship-tips_b_3175724.html

Judith, A. (1996). *Eastern body, Western mind: Psychology and the chakra system.* Berkeley, CA: Celestial Arts.

Klein, M. (2008). *America's war on sex: The attack on law, lust and liberty.* Westport, CT: Praeger.

Lowen, A. (1975). *Bioenergetics.* New York, NY: Penguin Compass.

Moore, T. (1990). *Dark eros: The imagination of sadism.* Woodstock, CT: Spring.

Morin, J. (1995). *The erotic mind: Unlocking the inner sources of sexual passion and fulfillment.* New York, NY: Harper Collins.

Neu, J. (2002). An ethics of fantasy? *Journal of Theoretical and Philosophical Psychology, 22*(2), 133-157. doi:10.1037/h0091219

No1 Reviews (2013). *A-Z list of BDSM/bondage fetish adult dating sites.* Retrieved from http://alternative-adult-dating-websites.no1reviews.com/sitemap.html

Paglia, C. (1990). *Sexual personae, art and decadence from Nefertiti to Emily Dickinson.* New Haven, CT: Yale Press.

Parker-Pope, T. (2008). *Love, sex and the changing landscape of infidelity.* Retrieved from http://www.nytimes.com/2008/10/28/health/28well.html

Perez, J. (2005). *The Spanish inquisition: A history.* New Haven, CT: Yale Press.

Phelan, J. E. (2009). Exploring the use of touch in the psychotherapeutic setting: A phenomenological review. *Psychotherapy: Theory, Research, Practice, Training, 46*(1), 97-111.

Salazar, C. (2006). Anthropology and sexual morality: A theoretical investigation. New York, NY: Berghahn Books.

Taylor, J. M. (2009). *Eros ascending: The life-transforming power of sacred sexuality.* Berkeley, CA: North Atlantic Books.

Wade, J. (2004). *Transcendent sex: When lovemaking opens the veil,* New York, NY: Pocket Books.

Williams, W. (2003). *Gay and lesbian rights in the United States: A documentary history.* New York, NY: Greenwood.

Zurbriggen, E. L., & Yost, M. R. (2004). Power, desire, and pleasure in sexual fantasies. *Journal of Sex Research, 41,* 288-300.

About the Author

As a sex-positive therapist and guide Galen has worked with hundreds of men, women and couples who've sought support to be honest and empowered in who they are sexually, and heal from the decades of fear, shame, trauma and harsh judgments that held their authentic desire back. He has a Master's degree in Transpersonal Psychology, with an emphasis on authentic sexual expression. He regularly presents at a variety of Sexuality related conferences and lectures at universities and grad schools on sex-positive psychological models.

Galen has been interviewed and written for numerous media such as Playboy radio, Mic, the Good Men Project and others for his innovative views and research on conscious sexuality and the nature of Fetishsexuality, aka Kink. He has been advocating for sex positive approaches to understanding the complex nature of sexual desire and active in the Sex-Positive Psychology, Fetish/Kink, and Conscious Sexuality communities since 1998. His private client practice is located in Portland, OR. In person, phone or Skype sessions can be arranged through his website GalenFous.com Look for his new book, *"Man on a Mission – defining your personal code of masculinity"* in the summer of 2016.

Take the **Discover Your Personal Erotic Myth Survey** at: www.GalenFous.com/PEM

ALSO BY GALEN FOUS

THE SHARP EDGE OF LOVE

The Sharp Edge of Love is a highly intelligent, passionate, edgy, authentic exploration of the mystery of female erotic submission (from their own point of view), written in prose that is elegantly real, and sharp as the thorns on a rose. The book reveals how erotic Dominance and submission plays out in a romantic encounter, and how the internet plays matchmaker - for better and for worse! These are all true accounts, with a dozen, highly compelling and well-crafted BDSM fictions with provocative, Dark Eros taboo woven throughout. Available on Amazon.

"...like eavesdropping on a private conversation... these intimate confessions made me blush and turned me on."

Betty Dodson, Ph.D,
Author of 'Sex for One'

"...I became literally obsessed, unable to keep my hands off the book – or myself!"

Cassandra Snow, Mindcaviar.com

"...a taboo-breakers stroke dream...like A Man and His Maid all over again, only without the British Victoriana."

Susie Bright, Playboy columnist;
Editor for 'Best American Erotica'

"I found the accurate portrayal of the D/s world, the blur of reality and fantasy, most compelling."

Deborah Hyde, Author of 'Pursed Lips,'
Novelist, Journalist, and Editor

"This book is a catharsis and a documentary – a must-read for anyone interested in Dominance and submission."

Erotic Readers Association

ADULT TOY DESIGN

The **Tetruss 3 in 1 Portable Dungeon Suspension Bondage Rig & Sex Swing**. The world's most versatile adult toy! Serving the global Fetish community since 2000. Tetruss.com

www.ingramcontent.com/pod-product-compliance
Lightning Source LLC
Chambersburg PA
CBHW030435290526

45786CB00001B/302

* 9 7 8 1 5 1 8 6 5 9 5 3 9 *